THE STORY OF
THE ROYAL HOSPITAL,
KILMAINHAM

ROYAL HOSPITAL

FAC-SIMILE OF THE
OLD BOOK PLATE
IN THE ROYAL HOSPITAL LIBRARY.

The Story of
THE ROYAL HOSPITAL,
KILMAINHAM

BY

MAJOR E. S. E. CHILDERS, R.E.
Assistant Military Secretary

AND

ROBERT STEWART

AMPLIFIED AND REPUBLISHED BY

CAPTAIN R. F. NATION,
ROYAL FUSILIERS
Assistant Military Secretary

LONDON: HUTCHINSON & CO.
:: *PATERNOSTER ROW* ::
MDCCCCXXI.

I hope that every visitor
to the Royal Hospital may
purchase a copy of this
Handbook. Whatever
is made by its sale will
be devoted to increase
the comforts of the old
Irish soldiers of the Queen
who live here.

Royal Hospital Wolseley
8th Sept. 1892 Genl.

The revision of this handbook has been undertaken in the hope that it may stimulate public interest in the old soldiers of the King, and in the historic building which is their home in Ireland.

Macready,
General.

30th Novr 1921.

CONTENTS

PART I

PART II

APPENDICES

The Story of the Royal Hospital, Kilmainham

PART I

CHAPTER I

FOUNDATION OF THE PRESENT HOSPITAL

ROUND few structures in Ireland gather such stores of interest, local and historical, as are found within the boundaries of the Royal Hospital at Kilmainham. As a building it has many claims to attention. It is well situated, its grounds commanding an attractive view of the Phœnix Park[1] on one side, and a fine prospect of the Dublin and Wicklow mountains on the other. The visitor will find an additional charm in the glimpses of garden, avenue lined with stately trees, and pleasant surroundings, while he contemplates the edifice itself, or examines its various objects of curiosity. Nor can it be supposed that his patriotism and humanity will allow but the least consideration to the old soldiers who have here their home.

A reviving interest has of late grown up in the worn-out veteran. To all who share in that interest some special acquaintance with this establishment will not be devoid of attraction. For over two hundred years shelter and comfort have here been afforded to his old age and feebleness. "We directed," runs the Charter of Charles the Second, "an Hospital to be erected near our City of Dublin, for the reception and Entertainment of such antient, maimed and infirm officers and soldiers ; to the end that such . . . as have faithfully served, or hereafter shall faithfully serve Us, our Heirs or Successors, in the Strength and vigour of their youth, may in the

---

[1] Phœnix Park—from the Irish words "Fein Ishke," clear spring.

Weakness and Disaster that their old Age, Wounds or other Misfortunes may bring them into, find a comfortable Retreat, and a competent maintenance therein."

Charles was doubtless not unwilling to entertain a project so likely to foster the fidelity and animate the zeal of those on whom so much would depend in an hour of crisis. The sentiments well befitted the sovereign from whose reign our historic regiments date their beginning.[1] He himself laid the first stone of Chelsea Hospital, the sister institution for soldiers on the English establishment, that at Kilmainham being intended for the army in Ireland only. It is not, however, to Charles that the chief credit is to be assigned for the erection of this latter Hospital, but to his Viceroy, the great Duke of Ormond.

The Earl of Ormond, as he then was, possessed the most gallant and attractive personality. When King Charles I. offered him the garter, about to become vacant by the attainder of the Earl of Strafford, Ormond declined the honour, saying that in his present difficulties the King might find it of use to win over or fix the adhesion of someone less steady than himself.

That very Strafford it was, who had first brought Ormond into prominence, when the former was Lord Deputy. An order had been issued by Strafford that members of the Irish Parliament should be disarmed previous to entering the Chamber. Ormond disregarded this, and, when checked in the most determined manner by Strafford and his sword demanded, answered, "If you have my sword it shall be in your guts." He justified his words by producing the King's writ, summoning him to come to Parliament " girded with a sword."

---

[1] 1st and 2nd Life Guards, Royal Horse Guards (formerly Lord Oxford's Regiment, hence " The Blues "), Grenadier Guards, and Coldstream Guards date from 1661; Scots Guards and 2nd Foot (The Queen's) 1662 ; 3rd Foot (The Buffs) 1665 ; 1st Foot (The Royal Scots) 1666 ; 5th Foot and 6th Foot were raised for the Dutch service in 1674 ; 21st Foot (Royal Scots Fusiliers) date from 1678 ; 4th Foot (The King's Own), 1680 ; 2nd Dragoons (Royal Scots Greys), 1681 ; 1st Royal Dragoons, 1683 ; 18th Foot (The Royal Irish) from about 1684.

Ormond was himself of semi-royal descent; James, Earl of Ormond, his ancestor, son of Edward le Botiller, espoused Eleanor Bohun, grand-daughter of Edward I.

In the intestine broils and devastating wars, caused by rival races, intolerant creeds, and convulsed politics, which had at the middle of the 17th century well nigh banished civilisation from Ireland, one prominent figure commands respect. No charge of idle cruelty, treacherous betrayal, dishonest purpose, or time-serving conduct, can fairly be made against James Duke of Ormond. For ten years, amid faction, misrule, and insurrection, he sustained with talent and fidelity the despairing cause of monarchy. A like period he spent in exile with his royal master. "It may not unusefully be remembered to the king," he writes, when Charles in later years listened to spiteful intrigues, "that no opposition or temptation ever frightened or allured me from my duty to the Crown." At the Restoration his services could not be overlooked. He regained his family estates, with large additional grants, while a dukedom and other honours were awarded him.

In 1662 he returned to Ireland as Lord Lieutenant, and held that position till 1668. He was again reappointed in 1677, and remained in the dignity till after the accession of James II. in 1685. His tenure of office was marked by a moderation to which tribute has been paid by the most biased writers. Though passions ran high, no serious outbreak is recorded in Ireland during the reign of Charles. No small part of the credit is due to the impartiality and the energy of Ormond.

Peace and security produced their fruits. Men " finding the ease and safety of living peaceably with their neighbours," turned their attention to useful labour and to trade. "Trade," writes Ormond, "was visibly increased of late years, and was reasonably expected to increase daily as the times grew more settled." Immense droves of cattle, "larger than the Scots breed," throve on the rich Irish pasture, and, exported in great numbers, were a source of jealousy and protection laws in both Scotland and

England. At Chapelizod[1] and Carrick the Duke established the linen manufacture, and worsted at Clonmel.

The army of about 7,000 men in the various garrisons were but becoming grey in ease and routine. Their Marshal, Arthur Earl of Granard, about 1675 found the question thrust upon him of some future subsistence for the many soldiers grown aged or otherwise unserviceable, but still continued in pay, " for want of some other fitting provision for their livelihood and maintenance."

Five years before, under similar circumstances, the ambitious King of France had completed the splendid edifice of the *Invalides* for his disabled warriors. It naturally suggested itself that something of the kind might be done here. The Earl of Essex, Lord Lieutenant, favoured the design, and accordingly some surveys to find suitable ground appear to have been made by his orders. But it was not till Ormond superseded him that the matter was taken energetically in hand. The necessity had naturally become more pressing. On 27th October, 1679, a letter was obtained from Charles authorising the erection of an Hospital.

Very likely financial difficulties had hitherto barred the way—

> " That eternal want of pence
> Which vexes public men."

These now disappeared. The Irish revenue received special attention from Ormond when he resumed the reins of government. He had gradually remedied a state of things in which " the Army and other branches of the Establishment," as he complained to the king, " seemed to be doomed to be in perpetual arrear." In the course of his efforts a sum of £36,500[2] had been obtained from " Robert and William Bridges, Gentlemen," to pay off the arrears due to the army. Part of this loan was repaid by an ingenious

---

[1] Chapelizod—a corruption of the words " Chapelle d'Yseult," and reputed to have been the home, at one time, of the mythical Yseult beloved of Tristram.

[2] No inconsiderable sum for those times, the Irish annual revenue being about £300,000.

Northern aspect of the House from within the courtyard, showing the exterior of the Great Hall, the Master's quarters, and the steeple.

[Facing page 12.

(and, to us, amusing) method. It was simply recharged on the pay of the troops by a deduction of twelve pence in the pound from all amounts becoming due to them for eighteen months. There was, however, nothing very harassing in this to men who for some time had been accustomed to give acquittances for their arrears on receiving two-thirds of the amount of their proper claim.

The arrangement with Messrs. Bridges had ceased on 29th March, 1679. From that date the rate of deduction was reduced by Charles' letter to sixpence, and ordered to be wholly applied to making a provision for aged and maimed officers and soldiers.

Soon after the receipt of the letter a committee was appointed by Order in Council to put the scheme into effect. Already the lands of Kilmainham, then included in the Phœnix Park, had been noted as suitable for the purpose in view. Of the ancient Priory there but remained " an old ruinous building, commonly called the Castle of Kilmainham." It was resolved to utilise the neglected grounds and inviting situation. The present site for the House was selected as being the highest and nearest the city. A model was designed by Sir Christopher Wren, and approved by the committee and the Lord Lieutenant.

On the 29th April, 1680, the ceremony of laying the first stone was performed by the Duke of Ormond before a large assemblage of the nobility and principal officers of the army. In less than four years the Hospital was completed as it stands to-day, with the exception of the steeple. This latter was added in 1701, as it was " first intended to be finished." An instructive account of the sums paid for the various classes of material and work is still preserved (see Appendix I.). The total cost was roughly about £24,000.

When the project was definitely settled in 1679, a return had been made of soldiers unfit for further service. About 300 such were found. Assuming a tenth of these would die every year, the Surveyor General considered that by providing accommodation for 300, the army would be for ever kept free in times of peace from disabled men, and the Hospital was constructed with this expectation. Dividing 30 (the number of vacancies which would on the above assumption occur every year in the Hospital) into 7,000 (the total number of troops in Ireland) and taking the quotient as the average term of life in years of a soldier, one indication may be noted of a delusion in the hope. Moreover, no regard was paid to a contemplated increase in the army, which had reached a strength of 11,000 men before the building was finished.

CHAPTER II

THE ANCIENT PRIORIES OF KILMAINHAM

In the name Kilmainham is perpetuated some evidence of the most ancient history of the locality. Saint Maignend and his " kil," or church—though it was but of wattle and clay—are thus commemorated for all times. It has been gleaned that he was the son of Aidus, Prince of Oriell (now Co. Louth), and that in 606 he was Abbot of a monastery here. This monastery flourished throughout the golden era of Irish history, and seems to have been an active centre of learning. The death of Leargus O'Fidhchain, " the philosopher of Kilmainham," is recorded by the Four Masters under the year 782.

Soon after this latter date the Danes began their incursions into Ireland. It is now satisfactorily established that these invaders were by no means the ferocious and ruthless savages which most historians represent them to have been. Their minds were, however, deeply imbued with a most bitter hatred of Christianity—a hatred due not only to the influence of their own superstition, but also deep-rooted by the national resistance which as a free people they had offered to Charlemagne's efforts at conversion by the sword. Before the year 840 they had established themselves at Dublin. No Christian community could any longer exist in the immediate vicinity of that city. Bells, matins, vespers; lectures in law, in divinity, in poetry, in history; copying and beautifying of manuscripts, ceased at Kilmainham. The fields of the desolated monastery became the favourite camping-ground of the Irish forces in their raids against the Danes of Dublin. Brian Boru's army lay here for some months in 1013,

and again, when reassembled in the following spring,
before the battle of Clontarf.

In 1174 the famous Richard Strongbow, Earl of Pem-
broke, erected a Priory for Knights Templars on the site
of the ancient Abbey. That society of ecclesiastical
warriors was then rapidly rising to the summit of its power
and fame. The prowess of the Templars was unrivalled,
while the sanctity of their lives was the admiration of the
Christian world. The lands of Kilmainham were bestowed
upon the Priory, and the grant confirmed by Henry the
second. An important accession of strength was thus
gained for the Anglo-Norman element in Ireland. The
Templars zealously lent their assistance in warding off
from Dublin the incursions of the Wicklow septs, and in
the perpetual warfare waged with the native princes.
Nor were even their skill and valour always sufficient
to decide the issue. At the Battle of Glyndelory, in 1274,
for instance, William Fitzroger, the Prior of Kilmainham,
was taken prisoner by the Irish, and many of his friars
were slain.

Besides Kilmainham, the Templars had several subor-
dinate establishments in Ireland. The office of Lord
Deputy was filled by William de Rosse, their Prior, in
1296, and again in 1301. In 1302 he was appointed Chief
Justice.

But upon the Continent the order had fallen into univer-
sal detestation. Wealth as well as honour had followed
upon that esteem originally acquired by the character and
valour of the Knights. When, however, their vows of
poverty and humility became idle words, all else disappeared
which had given them a peculiar lustre in the eyes of a
romancing world. They became even as other men ;
worse than others in contrast with their professions.

Philip, King of France, moved by envy and avarice,
supported by popular feeling and by the Pope, suppressed
the Order in his own country. Edward the Second followed
his example in England. A mandate for the same purpose
was sent to the Justiciary of Ireland ; and on the day after

the Feast of the Purification, in 1307, it was carried out. Gerald, fourth son of Maurice Lord of Kerry, the Grand Master, and the members of the Order were seized and imprisoned. In 1309 they were all confined in the fortress of Dublin Castle, and in the following year their lands and possessions granted to the Knights Hospitallers. The members of the unfortunate Order were brought to trial at Dublin in 1312. Three Dominicans were appointed judges ; Franciscans and Augustinians were among the witnesses ; and the ruin of the Knights Templars was confirmed. Some lenity, however, was shown towards them, and the manors of Kilcloghan, Crooke, and Kilbarry assigned for their support.

There is now no trace of the edifice at Kilmainham which then came into possession of the Knights Hospitallers. Its site was further to the west than the present house, and it is said to have been a spacious and elegant structure. The castle of the Templars at Clontarf, which remained in good preservation until sixty years ago, was probably of a similar, if inferior, design. The great window of the Chapel of the present Hospital testifies to the taste exhibited in the ancient building.

A more rigid discipline had preserved for the Knights Hospitallers, or Knights of St. John of Jerusalem, that regard which secured them against the misfortunes which overtook the Templars. They became still more important and influential in Ireland than the latter had been. The prior of Kilmainham sat as a baron in Parliament, which now began to be summoned as a counterpart of that in England. One of these Parliaments was held at the "Hospital of St. John" in 1317. Roger Outlawe became prior of the Hospital soon after that date. He was appointed Lord Chancellor in 1321, and became Lord Deputy in 1327. To Walter de Islip, who was Lord Treasurer of Ireland in 1315 and 1326, Outlawe granted the privilege of residence with other advantages in the Hospital. The terms of the grant, as extracted from Archdall's *Monasticon*, afford a rich picture of the old place, and are as follows :

B

"Prior Roger Outlawe granted to Master Walter Islip, during life, entertainment, for himself, two upper servants, a chamberlain and another servant, five boys and five horses. The said Walter to sit at the right hand of the prior thereby to be more commodiously served in eating and drinking. His chaplain to have a place at the table with the brethren of the house. That his ' pad ' and other horses should have the same forage with the prior's. That at the Feast of the Nativity, annually, he should have a gown and four garments of the better kind of cloth, the same as the prior's ; his chaplain clothed in like manner as the brethren, and his servants as those of the prior. That when he dined in his own apartments he should have three white loaves equal in goodness and size to the prior's ; ten flaggons of the best ale ; beef, mutton, and pork from the kitchen, raw or dressed as the prior was served, together with roast meat or soup. That with his servants and goods he should have ingress and egress through all gates and doors belonging to the priory. That he should have a proper place within the walls of the Castle near the Great Gate to build a stable for his horses, and part of the garden near the said gate to make a nursery. That whenever the said Walter should dine in the hall, or in the prior's chamber, he should be allowed for his evening potation after dinner, three flaggons of the best ale ; and that in the season of Lent and other times of fasting he should be served with flesh-meat as usual, except he chose to abstain from it."

Another touch may be added to this picture from a different source : " Alice Unred, relict of Roger Palmer, grants " [about the year 1335] " to Sir John Payn, chaplain, a messuage opposite the House of St. John the Baptist " . . . " at a yearly rent of 10s., payable to the prior and brethren of the Hospital of St. John, without the new gate, the chief lords thereof,"—wherein appears a distinct indication of the " ways and means " whereby flaggons of ale, beef, and other things became possible for the prior, the brethren, and their guests.

In 1329 a Bishop of Ossory, Richard Ledred, did not

disdain to prefer a charge of witchcraft against Alice Kettle and her son William. Prior Outlawe, as Lord Justice, showed some lenity to the prisoners. He was himself, in consequence, accused of heresy. On the meeting of parliament a committee was appointed to investigate the case. It was reported by them that the Lord Justice " was orthodox, a zealous champion of the faith, and ready to defend it with 'his life.'" The victor retorted the charge of heresy upon Ledred, and that prelate was obliged to make his escape from Ireland.

Under the guardianship of Outlawe the endowments of the Hospitallers were considerably augmented by fresh grants of land and churches. His interest stood high, as he often filled the office of Lord Deputy, and he is said to have been an able and judicious statesman. He died in 1340.

When Henry the Fifth beseiged Rouen, in 1418, the Prior of Kilmainham, Thomas le Botiller (Butler) brought a body of 1,600 Irish, "in mail, with darts and skeins," to his assistance. "They did so do their devoir," writes Hall, "that none were more praised, nor did more damage to their enemies." Their leader died upon this expedition.

The Hospitallers now began to fall into the errors which had subverted their predecessors, the Templars. The Visitor-General of the Order in 1447 removed Prior Thomas Fitzgerald from office at Kilmainham on account of mal-administration and avarice. When leaving the place Fitzgerald took with him the Hospital Seal, which he employed in some further bequests to himself. Upon petition from his successor, however, the parliament rendered his action illegal. But he was reinstated in office shortly afterwards through the influence of his faction, the great Geraldine family.

James Keating, who was made prior in 1461, distinguished himself above all the others by his rapacity, his audacity, and his address. He signalised his accession to office by an affray with Sir Robert Dowdal, Deputy to the Lord Treasurer, whom he assailed with a drawn sword upon the

Clonliffe road, while that official was proceeding on a pious pilgrimage to St. Glamokis. Keating was condemned in a fine of one hundred marks as he did not put in an appearance to answer for this offence, together with a like amount for compensation to Dowdal. But as he had happened at the time of trial to be in England upon the King's business, he contrived to escape the penalty altogether.

He took advantage of various irregularities in the actions of his two predecessors in office to obtain a decision that they had not been legal priors at all ; and that, consequently all assignments which they had made to the detriment of the Hospital should be annulled. In like manner he procured an act from the parliament confirming all privileges and gifts obtained by the priors and friars of Kilmainham since the time of King John, but declaring all grants made to their prejudice to be null and void.

Having been appointed Constable to the Castle of Dublin, Keating fortified it against the Lord Deputy, but was compelled to make submission. He then began to dissipate the treasures and property of the Hospital—selling some of the jewels, and pawning a piece of the true cross. At length the Grand Master of Rhodes ordered him to be deposed, and appointed Marmaduke Lumley, an Englishman, in his stead. But as soon as Keating learned that the new prior had landed at Clontarf, he hastened thither with a body of armed men, seized upon his rival, and constrained him to resign his patents of office. This outrage was followed by the excommunication of Keating. He revenged himself by depriving Lumley of the commandery of Kilseran, which that unfortunate man had been permitted to occupy, and putting him into prison. The authority of the Viceroy, owing to the Wars of the Roses in England, and the neglected state of Irish affairs, was inefficient for restraining these high-handed measures.

Keating supported the pretensions of Lambert Simnel to the throne of England. For that offence he was removed in 1488 from the office of Constable of the Castle of Dublin, but retained forcible possession of the Hospital. About

1491 he was finally expelled in disgrace, and is said to have ended his eventful career in extreme poverty.

Various measures were now taken by parliament to prevent a recurrence of such misdemeanours as had characterised Keating's term of office. The resources of the Hospital were recruited, and its alienated property restored. Yet the spirit of turbulence was not readily lost by men who had been trained by Keating. In 1506 the Prior of Kilmainham, Robert Evers, finding his establishment in lack of hay, made a raid upon some supplies which belonged to the Dominicans of the Friary of St. Saviour. The Mayor of the city hastened with some forces to the scene, and drove the aggressors into Kilmainham.

In 1535, amid the general dissolution of religious houses, the possessions of the Hospitallers in Ireland were surrendered to the King. Sir John Rawson, who had been prior since 1528, was thereupon created Viscount Clontarf, and granted a pension of five hundred marks from the Hospital revenues. The brethren of the fraternity likewise received pittances for their support.

In an interesting letter, from the Lord Deputy, recommending the grant of the Viscountcy to Sir John Rawson, it is stated that the Lord of Kilmainham "has been the person which, next your Majesty's Deputy, hath kept the best house, and English sort ; and at all times when strangers of other countries had repaired thither, feasted and entertained them to your highness's honour." It is also remarked that "he has given up several implements very necessary for the house, with corn, hay, and other things whereof I had need ; and also hath caused the principal house there to be well and substantially repaired in all places needful, which assuredly is a goodly house, and great pity that it should decay."

In the reign of Queen Mary the establishment was allowed to be reconstituted by Cardinal Pole, and Sir Oswald Massingberd was appointed prior in 1557. He held office until the second year of Queen Elizabeth's reign.

The Crown then reasserted its claims to ownership, and Massingberd retired abroad.

The place was occasionally occupied by the Irish Viceroys as a residence for some time longer. It was then handed over to the care of Keepers. Beverly Newcomen, the last Keeper, resigned his trust in 1617, and this ancient seat of pomp and power was then allowed to fall gradually into decay.

There is a hollow in the Master's Fields to the west of the present house, along the crest of which the ancient buildings ran. The eye may follow what appear to be the traces of foundations, but if this is so, it is indeed but a faint mark of what was once the lordly Priory.

CHAPTER III

BULLY'S ACRE AND ST. JOHN'S WELL

WITHIN the boundaries of the Royal Hospital there is one monument of antiquity whose memories are specially varied and interesting. It is said to mark the last resting-place of distinguished Irish chieftains who were slain at the battle of Clontarf, and amongst these are included Murrough and Turlough, the son and grandson of Brian Boru, who, next to Brian himself, are the popular heroes of the great victory.[1] According to the Munster book of battles by MacLiag, Prince Murrough was buried at the west end of St. Maignend's Church, a long stone, on which his name was written, marking his tomb.

There now remains but the shaft (about 10 feet high) of what must have been a large cross, which may originally have been the " termon " or boundary cross of St. Maignend's monastery.

This shaft is of coarse granite, and upon the western side of it is graven a true lover's knot, said really to be an ancient emblem of eternity—sculpture of the eleventh century, not later—which can be readily followed by the finger or observed with the eye when the sunlight falls at a proper angle. Some letters or symbols are also apparent on the opposite side, but they have not yet been deciphered or explained.

[1] Brian Boru, the Irish hero, who defeated the Danes in this memorable battle, was slain in the encounter, together with his son and grandson, but though Murrough and Turlough are believed to have been brought to Kilmainham and buried before the great cross there, there is nothing to substantiate Sir John Traill's statement that Brian Boru's grave was there also. Tradition has it that he was buried at Armagh (*see* p. 26).

At one time "the cross of Kilmaynan by the bounds of the lands of Kilmaynan " served to mark the extent of the liberties of Dublin in this direction, as appears from a charter granted by King Richard the Second to the city. From thence the Mayor and his officers, in their annual progress, "rode downward to Bow Bridge, passing under an arch of the same through the water of Cammock "—though " for their more ease they sometimes rode through the Prior of Christ Church his lands." Several references are also made to the "great cross of Kilmainham " in various other documents relating to the city. Its site is now included in the Hospital cemetery so well known in the popular traditions of Dublin as Bully's Acre.

By an inquisition taken of the Priory of Kilmainham in the thirty-second year of the reign of Henry VIII. it appears that the Kilmainham possessions consisted of a messuage, called the Castle-House, three parks and an acre adjacent called the Bayl-Yard : as an office existed among the ancient knights called bailiff, it is thought that he had charge of that part where Bully's Acre is situated, and so corrupted to Bully from Baily. The ordinary derivation of the name is from its having been a place where pugilists decided their quarrels, and called from thence the Bully's Acre. It contains three acres and a half (old Irish measure).

The burying-ground which has earned this remarkable appellation will naturally be presumed to be notable for something else besides the presence of one historic monument. And it is so in fact : Bully's Acre has a history peculiarly its own.

It would appear to have been used as a repository for the dead since the time of St. Maignend. What an interesting register, were it in existence, of Irish monk, Irish prince, Knight Templar, and Knight Hospitaller, who have there been laid to rest !

In the neglect of the Kilmainham lands which ensued upon their possession by the Crown, the ancient cemetery came more and more into use amongst those who reverenced the memories of the Abbey of St. John. And when the

Royal Hospital was erected this privilege of sepulchre within its bounds does not appear to have been interfered with.

The most ancient monument which is still legible is a simple headstone inscribed "Here lieth the body of Hive Hacket and Elizabeth Hacket who died the year 1652." Who these worthies were is not known, but the stone goes to prove the preceding assertion that Kilmainham was used by the populace as a burying-ground, between the time that the last Keeper left the ancient Priory to its ruin in 1617, and its re-birth in its present form in 1680.

Besides the interest which consequently centred in Bully's Acre as their chief burying-place, many of the people of Dublin, as well as multitudes from other quarters, found a greater attraction there in the presence of a holy well. Across the junction of St. John's Road with the Circular Road there still sometimes flows from Bully's Acre a tiny stream. It indicates the whereabouts of the springs which supplied the well of St. John—"the Siloam of Kilmainham once," says Burton, "now a neglected rill. Beside it, in days of yore, the Asiatic templar spake of Jerusalem, and laved his hands."

In the month of June, 1737, a complaint was made by the officers of the Hospital that their grazing fields were rendered almost useless owing to the traffic through them to "a well near Kilmainham frequented by numbers of superstitious persons."

The Feast of St. John the Baptist occurs on the 24th June, and upon that day the waters of the spring were supposed to possess special virtues for the purification of sin and disease. It is moreover at the middle of summer, and if the weather were propitious scant shelter might suffice for the day or night. With a people at once gay, careless, and devout, the natural consequences followed. A scene of piety mixed with revelry, debauchery, and dissipation came to be exhibited year after year. "The fields," says the contemporary record, "are generally by day and night full of idle and disorderly people ; the grass is trod down ; the cattle stray." At an alehouse, too, the Black Lion, erected by a man named Flanagan on the brink of the well, a roaring trade was doubtless carried on.[1]

A way leading from the city had been opened across the north side of the Hospital lands for the convenience of the Earl of Galway, a Lord Justice, when he dwelt at Island Bridge. This, it was stated, had been made into a common thoroughfare, and afforded access for the multitudes into the fields near the well. Repeated attempts to stop it up proved futile. Walls and gates erected in the daytime were levelled by the populace at night. The plan was therefore adopted of farming out Bully's Acre and the adjoining fields. They were obtained by a dairyman and publican named Cullen, of Gallow's Hill. He contrived to exercise some kind of control over the lands, and exacted a fee of from 3d. to 1d. for each burial, according to the size of the coffin and the circumstances of the parties concerned ; but of course he in no way discountenanced the gay vigils which tended directly to his own profit as a publican.

Things went on in this fashion until General Dilkes became Master of the Hospital in 1755. " He endeavoured," says Sir John Traill, " to put a stop to the pernicious nocturnal revels. He applied to the magistrates, who frequently attended and dispersed them, and he completely enclosed the burying-ground by walls. He levelled the graves and removed the headstones. This had the desired effect. The frequent compliments to departed friends, by decorating their graves with garlands, and the worshipping of Brien's supposed monument ceased. These objects of respect and adoration being removed, St. John's Well lost much of its wonted powerful attraction, and the burying-ground remained perfectly shut up for some years."

After this success, General Dilkes wished further to recover for the Hospital the control of the road which led

---

[1] The South Circular Road was not made until about 1775. It should therefore be conceived as replaced by a continuation of Bully's Acre in reading the above account.

through the fields to Island Bridge, and erected gates across it. But it had long been enjoyed as an open thoroughfare by the public. Men of property took up the popular cause. Subscriptions were raised, and the opinion of eminent counsel obtained. Application was made to the Grand Jury of the county, who presented that the gates were a common obstruction and public nuisance. This presentment was traversed by the Governors of the Hospital, but it was sustained by the verdict of the King's Bench. An immense multitude had waited the result outside the court-house. Immediately it was made known, they set off with pickaxe and crowbar to vindicate their rights. But General Dilkes had already removed the gates in anticipation of any such proceeding. Being thus deprived of a much-expected pleasure, the mob raised a cry of " Down with the wall of Bully's Acre ! " This work of destruction, at once so congenial to their instincts, and so agreeable to their prejudices, was soon completed. And thus Bully's Acre again became a common-land and was devoted to the same incongruous purposes as of yore.

The burial ground, thus exposed and neglected, was soon in a fearful condition. In 1769, upon remonstrance from the Grand Jury of the County, the Governors ordered the walls to be rebuilt. This, however, could not be accomplished, owing to the determined opposition of the populace. General Dilkes' life was threatened, if the work were not stopped, and application was formally made, by the Governors to the Lord Lieutenant, for protection. One serious attack appears to have been made about this time upon the Hospital itself.[1] It was headed by

[1] The account by Burton of the incidents which led to this attack appears to be very highly imaginative. He traces it to a love affair in which a Sergeant from the Hospital and the leader of the " Liberty Boys " were rivals. The Liberty Boys were the war-like youth of the Liberties of Dublin, formerly known as Rathland, who armed themselves to combat the periodical raids of the O'Byrnes and O'Tooles, which occurred as late as 1750. These Liberty Boys, in spite of the fact that their weapons were often of the most primitive description, obtained a reputation for valour by successfully defeating the marauders on several occasions, and driving them back to their mountain fortresses.

the " Liberty Boys," a band of roysterers hailing from the
Coombe. They burst in the western gate, which the sentry,
alarmed at the formidable gathering, had continued to
close, but not without being himself seriously injured.
He gave the alarm, and the more active of the pensioners
were speedily gathered and armed. Headed by General
Dilkes, these proceeded down the elm walk to oust the
rioters. "What a mob will do knows no man, least of all
themselves," says one who studied their qualities. On the
present occasion, however, they were opposed to men
who had seen service at Dettingen, Minden, and the
Heights of Abraham. A critical moment soon came.
Finding his men assailed with all the dangerous, if primitive, weapons of lawlessness and threatened by an occa-
sional musket shot, the General ordered his front line to
fire. The leader of the rioters fell dead, and a number
of others were wounded. A hasty flight of " Liberty
Boys " ensued. This unfortunate occurrence doubtless
deepened the current of popular feeling against the
enclosing of Bully's Acre, and it was eventually deemed
more prudent to abandon the design.

No further attention was paid to the graveyard until
the year 1795, when its woeful condition was at length
again taken notice of by the County Grand Jury. They
presented a sum of money towards the expenses of a new
wall. The legal title of the Governors to the control of
the disputed ground was investigated and declared perfectly valid. A better spirit prevailed in all quarters.
The privilege of free burial was continued, but interments
were placed under proper supervision. The wall was
erected ; the so-called monument of " Brian Boru " set up
again ; and a stone fountain provided on the edge of the
South Circular Road for the waters of St. John.

A few years later the body of Robert Emmet was buried
in Bully's Acre. No headstone, no tradition, points out
the spot of interment. There is some dispute, however,
as to whether the grave was not afterwards opened and
the remains conveyed to St. Michan's.

Western aspect of the House from the long avenue.

[*Facing page* 28.

The grave of another popular hero, of much humbler claims, but at one time of equal celebrity, is well distinguished. Few Irishmen past the age of fifty but were familiar in their youth with stories and ballads respecting Dan Donnelly. No spot on the Curragh of Kildare is better known than Donnelly's Hollow. For there the representatives of Ireland and England, namely, Donnelly and Cooper, met in a far-famed pugilistic encounter, and the Irishman was victorious. When he died some years after, it was thought fitting by the multitude that he should be honoured with that grave and monument commonly supposed to be Brian Boru's. "The tomb of Murrough," says the better informed *Dublin Penny Journal* (1832), "received the mortal remains of Dan Donnelly; and the victor of Clontarf and the victor of Kildare sleep in the same grave. We remember well his triumphal entry into Dublin after his great battle on the Curragh. That indeed was an ovation. He was borne on the shoulders of the people, his mother, like a Roman matron, leading the van in the procession, and, with all the pride of a second Agrippina, she frequently slapped her naked bosom, exposed for the occasion, and exultingly exclaimed— ' There's the breast that suck'd him ! '—' there's the breast that suck'd him ' ! ! ! "

Bully's Acre was finally closed as a public cemetery in 1832. Whoever curiously examines the tombstones will observe how many date from that year. For in the frightful pestilence of cholera which then raged, no less than five hundred interments took place here within ten days. The ground having " been for some ages the last home of the poor inhabitants of Dublin," was thus so dangerously overcrowded that nothing less than madness could permit the continuance of burials. A notice prohibiting such was accordingly issued by the Governors of the Hospital.

The observance of St. John's day at the Sacred Spring had, too, by that time, fallen into popular disfavour, and about 1844 the stone fountain erected in 1795 had to give place to the Great Southern and Western Railway. On the west side of the South Circular Road an arched recess in the wall still affords a supply of the once venerated water. It was constructed in lieu of the stone fountain, and was practically the last compliment paid to the virtues of St. John's Well.

Separated from Bully's Acre by the Western avenue is the "officers' burying-ground," appropriated in accordance with its title. It was once used for all inmates of the Hospital. Its most ancient tombstone, which bears a legible inscription, reads thus : " Corporal William Proby, who died 28th July, 1700." Burton speaks of him as " a hero, by tradition, of Ormond's wars ; a musketeer at Baggotrath ; and after (*sic*) crossed Boyne's flood ; wounded at Schomberg's side." He had been only admitted to the Hospital seven weeks before his death. Space forbids further details of the other interesting memorials in this quiet and secluded spot—

> " Where, like an infant's smile, over the dead
> A light of laughing flowers along the grass is spread,
> And grey walls moulder round, on which dull Time
> Feeds, like slow fire upon a hoary brand."

Two small enclosures on the northern side of Bully's Acre are enclosed by walls and set apart for the old soldiers of the Hospital. Beneath the simple mounds formerly marked by iron numbered tablets of shamrock form, and now by simple white marble headstones, they are laid to rest with military honours, as to each in his turn from age, wounds, or infirmity, is brought a last release.

May there long be found shelter and comfort in this Institution for those who have served, as they have done, the greatest Empire of the age.

View of the House from the west, showing the Master's quarters.

[Facing page 30.

CHAPTER IV

DESCRIPTION OF THE PRESENT HOSPITAL

THE prettier approach to the Royal Hospital is from the South Circular Road, on the west. On that side a gateway, surmounted by a Norman tower, affords access to a handsome avenue leading to the House. This tower is called the Richmond Tower, having originally been erected in the year 1812, during the viceroyalty of the Duke of Richmond. It first stood beside Barrack (formerly Bloody) Bridge in the city, but was removed to its present site in 1846. (See towards end of Chapter VI.)

A sentry paces up and down just inside. Aged elms lining the grass margins meet their arms across the carriage way. Walls rise on either hand—over that to the left lies the once notorious "Bully's Acre," while the old burying-ground of the institution is on the right. Neat hedges flank the second half of the way with a stretch of meadow land northwards. The west front of the House is presented gradually to view from behind the trees and bushes.

Perhaps, however, the place will more usually be reached by coming round the Kingsbridge Station of the Great Southern and Western Railway. Near at hand is the Infirmary with a residence for the physician and surgeon. The road which strikes off past these—bordered on the right by a large field with rows of trees—should be taken. A long narrow-roofed edifice, seen to the left 150 yards away on passing the Infirmary, was erected by the money and consecrated by the severe wit of Swift.

" He gave the little wealth he had
To build a house for foo_ and mad,
To show by one satiric touch
No nation needed it so much."

The eye will scarcely rest with pleasure on the environs
thereabouts. But a fairer spectacle lies ahead, where
behind a mass of foliage the Hospital is hidden—its steeple
alone to be seen—or, it may be, showing through waving
branches which autumn has left fantastic and bare. Passing on—through the gate, upon whose piers stand military
trophies,[1] by the magazine rifle and fixed bayonet of the
sentry, and up a short incline with banks of shrubs and
flowers—an open space soon is reached where the whole
east front is seen.

A house somewhat antique in appearance will attract
notice on the right hand. It is the residence of the Deputy
Adjutant-General of the Army in Ireland, who is also
ex-officio Deputy Master of the Hospital. Opposite it,
across two squares of lawn, is a large substantial looking
building, the house of the Chief General Staff Officer of
the Irish Command ; this house was built as the office
of the then Adjutant-General and was used as such until
the offices of G.H.Q. Irish Command were transferred in
1913 to the Old Military Infirmary Buildings in Parkgate
Street.

The Royal Hospital extends 306 feet from north to
south and 288 feet from east to west. The pile is continuous
along the four sides of a quadrangle. Massive, uniform, and
relieved by a moderate diffusion of ornament, it impresses
the beholder with a sense of completeness. Utility and
architectural effect have been quietly and happily combined.

The north front, facing the Liffey and the Phœnix
Park, is the principal one.[2] Here are the Chapel, its
eastern wing ; the Great Hall in the middle ; and the

[1] These armorial trophies formerly stood in the wide, open space
before the eastern doorway leading into the courtyard of the house.

[2] This part of the Hospital is kept private. The public had a
free thoroughfare round the south side, which has had to be curtailed
for safety since the troublous days of the Irish Rebellion of 1916.

Carved wooden panel above the northern entrance to the House.

Carved wooden panel above the southern entrance to the House.

[*Facing page* 32.

apartments of the Commander of the Forces in Ireland (who is the Master of the Hospital) along its western part.[1] From its centre projects the great entrance for 17½ feet by 66 feet, leading into the Great Hall, and presenting an ornamental front of the Corinthian order. This mainly consists of an angular pediment supported by four pilasters, a large circular-headed window being disposed between each outer pair, the doorway between the inner pair. The doorway, reached by a flight of stone steps, is likewise adorned by a pilaster on each side with a semicircular pediment superposed, above which again the arms of the Duke of Ormond are sculptured in stone. A beautifully worked festoon of flowers, entwining a human head, decorates the wooden panel above the door.

Over this entrance rises the steeple. Its lower storey is square and plain, with a Gothic window on each side, and surmounted by a plain entablature having urns upon its four corners. The second storey, of smaller dimensions, contains the clock, furnished with a dial for each wall. An octagonal spire, terminating in a ball and vane, completes the whole.

Five windows similar to those of the central projection, but larger, extend along each of the two portions into which it divides this exterior. Above those on the right other windows rise out of the roofing, a mode of lighting the upper storey which is continued around the other sides and gives a distinctive character to the building.

The north front is of stone, but is now rough-cast in common with the rest of the building. The other fronts are of brick. They are three storeys high. At the centre

[1] In the garden belonging to the Commander of the Forces, which is a fine walled garden below and immediately to the north of the north front of the hospital, there is a mulberry tree which was planted by James II. In a secluded corner lie buried the remains of Lord Robert's well-known white Arab charger, Vonolel, decorated by H.M. Queen Victoria with the Afghan War Medal and Cabul-Khandahar Star and her Jubilee Medal. Here also you will find a stone to another less known, but no doubt not less beloved, quadruped, Grey Alma, probably the trusted friend of some former resident of the Hospital.

of each there is an arched gateway. The panels above the gates display rich and carefully worked designs—those on the east and west of military trophies, while on the south, festoons of flowers and a lion's head match that over the northern door.

Some resemblance to the Hotel des Invalides may be traced in the east front, largely due to the grand window of the Chapel which rises above the roof at its northern end. No variation modifies the quaint simplicity of the front on the south. The west front exhibits no fresh peculiarity, except the porch of the Commander of the Forces' quarters near its northern extremity.

The handsome courtyard enclosed, of 210 feet square, is prettily laid out in grass plots. These are divided off by walks crossing from the entrances.

> " But entred in, a spacious court they see,
> Both plaine, and pleasaunt to be walked in."

A piazza, 13 feet wide, along three sides and part of the fourth, affords a covered passage to the Chapel. It is fronted by 59 arches, in the Italian manner, having a span each of 11 feet.

About the doorway of the Great Hall, in the centre of the north range, some features of the grand entrance on the exterior opposite are reproduced. There are the pediment above, pilasters to each side, the great windows, sculptured panel above the door, and the stone steps. An ancient sundial within the pediment, of the date 1748, modestly rivals the clock of the Tower.

The Great Hall

Merely to see the Great Hall will well repay the trouble of a visit to the Hospital. This noble apartment is 100 feet in length, 50 in breadth. Its lofty ceiling is divided into compartments of rectangular or circular form, which, however, are now somewhat hidden by a more modern arrangement of joists. The upper part of the walls is decorated with 22 portraits of sovereigns and Irish statesmen—among which are included King Charles the Second;

Western end of the Great Hall, showing the portrait of the Royal Founder above the fireplace.

Facing page 34.

William the Third, and Queen Mary ; Queen Anne, and her Consort, Prince George of Denmark ; James Duke of Ormond, the Founder. The portraits of the Sovereigns were bought at various times by the Governors ; that of King Charles II. is claimed to be by the hand of the famous Sir Godfrey Kneller. The portraits of the remaining personages were presented mostly by themselves. That of the Duke of Ormond is said to be an original painting, but the authorship is unknown. (See Appendix II.) These interesting and valuable memorials of illustrious person-ages are set off by an array of standards upon whose faded silks the spectator may read romance at will. (See Appendix III.) The lower half of the walls is wainscoted with oak, and displays armour, muskets, swords, old pistols, etc., fancifully arranged. (See Appendix IV.)

In an alcove forming part of the great entrance, the original Charter granted by Charles the Second, bearing the Royal sign manual and the great seal, is preserved for inspection. It is in perfect condition. A sheet of paper attached thereto exhibits the following true legend :

The Original Charter of the
Royal Hospital of Kilmainham,
Granted by H.M. King Charles II.
Lost on its removal to England A.D. 1688.
It was found among some family papers where it
had been lying for upwards of a century and was
Restored to the said Hospital, A.D. 1848,
By Edward Worth Newenham, Esqre.,
late of H.M. IXth Regt. of Foot,
As a token of his unfeigned respect for its
Gallant Inmates.

A small library of old books, mostly dating from the latter end of the 17th and the beginning of the 18th century, is also preserved here, and includes some valuable works.[1] In a second alcove another library of more recent books is kept for the use of the In-Pensioners.

The fine old fireplace at the west end perhaps deserves a mention as a spot of supreme interest to the old men. Here through the winter or on wet days they enjoy their

[1] A facsimile of the ancient bookplate of the Royal Hospital is given facing the title-page.

well-earned ease with draughts, newspapers, exchange of reminiscences, or the settlement of the nation's foreign and domestic policy. The visitor should not miss a close scrutiny of the medals displayed in glass cases as appropriate ornaments of this place of much resort. (See Appendix V.)

The east end is superbly ornamented in woodwork, and has a doorway at the middle opening into the chapel. Above this doorway are the Royal Arms, richly coloured, and decorated with flags.

The Chapel

The Chapel, which was consecrated in January, 1686, and dedicated to the memory of King Charles, the martyr, is oblong in shape, as were most ancient churches.[1]

As the visitor passes from the great hall into this beautiful House of God he will doubtless first be shown a fine gate of wrought iron, drawn across behind the door; it bears the royal cipher of Queen Anne, and is said to have been presented by her.

Overhead, on entering, is a small gallery furnished with a handsomely carved canopied pew formerly occupied by the master.

The range of windows along the north side is ornamented with stained glass, exhibiting in the centre the arms of various dignataries.

The great Gothic window which occupies the east end is of particular interest. The stone tracery and beautiful stained glass therein belonged to the church of the Knights Hospitallers, having been carefully removed and re-erected here, and being the last and, with the exception of parts of the masonry in the walls, the only portion of the ancient Priory which remains.

Whoever has a weakness for old times and old ways will not be displeased to hear that the style in which the old glass of the St. Catherine's wheel is stained cannot be

[1] Built, so antiquarians say, to represent an ark or ship tossed by the waves of this troublesome world. Hence the term " nave," from " navis," a ship.

View from the north, showing the whole of the north front, the Master's quarters being on the right and the Chapel on the left. The Master's garden is in the foreground and the Deputy Master's house detached on the left.

[Facing page 36.

equalled by the chemists and machinery of these days. But he will, no doubt, also admire the modern work in the lower part of the window; and it, too, does not lack cherished association, in that it was presented by Queen Victoria to commemorate Her Majesty's visit on the 7th August, 1849. Beneath this window is the Communion Table.

The Hospital possesses a large folio Church Bible of great historic interest, presented by Charles II., which monarch also gave to the Chapel certain beautiful pieces of Communion plate.

The angles of the chancel are adorned by beautiful carving in Irish oak; the lover of fine art will scrutinise this carving more carefully as the work of that supreme artist, Grinling Gibbons.

Within the altar rails stand two finely carved antique chairs presented by the Duke of Connaught, and without stands a lectern presented in December, 1901, by Masters, Deputy Masters, and Governors past and present, and others connected with the Royal Hospital—

"To the glory of God and in memory of the Hon. F. H. S. ROBERTS, V.C., Lieut. King's Royal Rifle Corps, who fell in a gallant attempt to save the guns at Colenso, 15th December, 1899."

There are various memorial tablets affixed to the walls.

"In memory of the Officers, non-commissioned Officers and men of the 16th Lancers who were killed in action, or died while serving with the Heavy Camel Corps in the Soudan, 1884-5.

Capt. Viscount St. Vincent.[1]	Pte. T. Taylor.
Lieut. W. B. Browne.	,, H.A. Sylvester.
Cpl. T. Livesay.	, , R. W. Osbourne.
Lce.-Cpl. A. Jacques.	,, W. Benstead.
	,, Thompson.

"Erected by their comrades, Officers, non-commissioned Officers, and men, 16th Lancers."

"In memory of John Joseph Corrigan (Captain), 3rd Dragoon Guards, who died at Melbourne, 6th January, 1866, aged 35 years, eldest son of Sir Dominic Corrigan, Bart. This Tablet is erected by his brother Officers, as a mark of their respect and esteem."

[1] Lord St. Vincent had in the ranks of his squadron a man destined to rise from the rank of trooper to that of Field-Marshal. He took particular interest in this man, and helped to lay the foundation of the military knowledge which enabled Sir William Robertson to rise from the lowest to the highest rank in the Service, a feat never before performed in the British Army.

" In memory of the late Staff Surgeon William Carte, J.P., 41 years Physician and Surgeon, Royal Hospital, Kilmainham. Erected by his Widow and Children."

" In loving memory of Frederick Hugh Sherston Roberts, V.C., Lieutenant, King's Royal Rifle Corps, only surviving son of Field-Marshal Lord Roberts and Nora his wife."

Attention being directed to the ceiling, the eye will range with pleasure over the richest of stucco work—designs of fruit, flowers, and so forth, which ornament a fanciful arrangement of geometrical figures. This work, designed by Cipriani, is said to be unmatched in the United Kingdom.

Divine Service is performed by the Chaplain of the Hospital. There is no organ, but ways and means are now being studied to make good this deficiency. In normal times the music is supplied by a Military Band, and a detachment of the soldiers from the neighbouring barracks attends the Sunday morning service in addition to the pensioners. Many civilians are wont to come to the bright, cheerful service, but space is rather limited. The dimensions of the Chapel are 86 feet by 36. The visitor can leave by a second doorway, direct to the piazza.

Arrangement of the Rest of the Building

About forty of the pensioners, who require special medical care, and are unfit for going up and down stairs, occupy a number of the rooms off the piazza. A large brass plate on the door of one of these bears the following interesting inscription :

By Permission of
Lt.-Genl. the Right Honble. Sir Edward Blakeney,
G.C.B. and G.C.H.
Master,
This plate has been inscribed by the non-commissioned officers and privates
of the Royal Hospital, to record their deep sense
of the condescension of
Her Most Gracious Majesty the Queen Victoria
In having personally visited this room on the 7th Augt., 1849,
accompanied by H.R.H. Prince Albert,
Thereby evincing the kind interest taken by these
Royal Personages
In the veteran inmates of this noble Institution.

Carved wooden panel above the western entrance to the House.

Carved wooden panel above the eastern entrance to the House.

[*Facing page* 38.

A chapel for the Roman Catholic inmates has been fitted up at the south-west angle.

Permission can be readily obtained for visiting the other floors of the house. Fine broad staircases lead to a splendid wide corridor on the first floor. Most of the rooms off this floor are assigned as quarters to officers who have the privilege of residence. The staircases continued to the second floor also lead to a wide corridor. About seventy of the more robust pensioners are quartered in the rooms in this part.[1]

[1] About twenty-four on the average are inmates of the Infirmary.

CHAPTER V

EARLY HISTORY

ON 26th March, 1684, the following persons were "entered and constituted officers of the said House with their several salaries":

	Per annum
Colonel John Jeffreys, Master, £300 per annum, Fee, and £200 for a Table	
James Gilbert, Chaplain	£80
Henry Gascoine, Treasurer	80
William Robinson, Auditor and Registrar ...	50
Arthur Dykes, Aid-Major	10
David Williams, Reader (to be in full orders and approved of by the Archbishop of the Diocese)	20
——— Surgeon	50
——— Surgeon's Mate	20
Peter Goodwin, Providore	30
Daniel Lyford, Butler	10
Paul Hogg, Cook, with Fees	20
William White, Gardener	16
Patrick Neyles, Chapel Keeper ...	8
Nathaniel Lake, Yeoman of Fuel ...	8
Richard Bevin, Do. Chambers ...	8

Ten servants to assist and attend the officers, £5 per annum each.

Women to wash and attend the sick, £15 per annum, without diet.

Well equipped with the above staff, the Hospital began its good work by admitting seventeen soldiers as a guard. These were provided with diet at the rate of 4d. per diem each, and with a money allowance of 6d.

a week. Their names, ages, and regiments are all entered in the careful and beautiful penmanship of the old book which begins the records.

Shortly after this the Board appointed a Committee of eight (three to be a quorum), to draw up rules and orders ; provision was made to prevent imposition, by requiring petitioners to bring certificates from the Muster Master-General or other proper authority ; the establishment fixed at 10 officers and 100 soldiers ; and the grazing of the land let to Richard Cullen. It being observed that the honour of the house " doth much depend upon the decent ordering of the tables, especially the Master's " an order was made for an increase of this officer's allowance to £300 to keep his own plentifully supplied, " to which all gentlemen, strangers, and others may be invited, that come to see the House."

And thus business is done from time to time, not at all in such a stupid fashion as might be supposed likely nearly two hundred and fifty years ago. Presently, indeed, the governors are desired by their Committee to strike out all such salaries and expenses as may be most conveniently spared. It is intended to raise the number of men provided for in the Hospital to 200. The revenue has been exhausted by the purchase of necessary furniture ; and several old men have been turned out of the army who have been *pensioned* on half-pay from the Hospital revenue. Accordingly, as the Master is in England, his table expense is struck off ; the gardener's salary is discontinued till there be occasion to use him ; some of the other salaries are taken off or suspended ; the grazing is again offered to whoever will give most for it ; and some honest officer or soldier is required to see that the providore, butler, cook, and fueller do not indulge in waste and extravagant expense.[1]

[1] One order of this period by the Committee—The Earl of Roscommon, Lord Lieutenant ; Sir Charles Fielding ; Abraham Yarner, Esq. ; Major Rupert Billingsley, begins—"Whereas the Cooke of the Hospitall hath hitherto taken to his own use the Suett, Fatt, Chops of Mutton, &c., under the pretense of Fees due to him, to the prejudice of the House, which in the year amounts to A considerable sume."

On 17th January, 1686, it is ordered that the Archbishop of Dublin be desired to consecrate the chapel " upon Wednesday next, and that the same be dedicated to the memory of King Charles I., Martyr."

The next interesting achievement by the Board, a very business-like one, evidently, was the settlement of the dietary allowance. It stands as follows for the soldiers and under-officers :—" To be supplied by the Providore at the rate 1¾d. per diem for each man.

Monday—Mutton and Broath.
Tuesday—Mutton, Veale, or Lamb, roast
Wednesday—Pease and Butter.
Thursday—Beef, boyled.
Friday—Fish, as the season requires.
Saturday—Burgooe.
Sunday—Beefe, roast.

Each man having a pound of meat after drest, and of the rest diett, a sufficient allowance over and above Broath and Water Gruel and Stirabout, constantly made every day for the sick at the Infirmary and Hospitall."[1]

Each man was also to be supplied with 18 ozs. of bread daily by the butler, at the rate of £5 per week for 217 men.

In February of the same year (1686), it is decided, after considering the humble petition of Mrs. Frances Goodwin for washing all manner of linen and attending the sick men in the Infirmary, that she shall receive £150 per annum for these services. In May, Charles Thompson is settled with for Medicines at the rate of £20 a year since the opening of the Hospital.

But while the Institution is being thus ordered, settled, and arranged, a storm has gathered round it. The records show the Duke of Ormond to have been present at meetings of the Governors held in Dublin Castle in the later months of 1684 and the beginning of 1685. But he was no favourite with the heir to the throne, who then, in the feeble condition of Charles, controlled public affairs. Before the

---

[1] This clumsy sentence, probably copied originally from a rough draft, can, it is hoped, with some patience, be understood by the reader.

brief and clear recital of the principal events of that stirring period, so far as they concerned the Hospital, and which was evidently written as soon as its affairs had been restored to their accustomed footing.

It appears that Tyrconnell resolved to " New Model " the army in Ireland upon lines which should be more acceptable to his gracious master. He found, however, that the Charter of the Royal Hospital expressly forbade any " Papist " to have share or lot in the matter. He desired to reverse the situation under form of law. Accordingly, the whole difficulty was submitted to Lord Chancellor Fitton. That acute man—" turning the case as a lawyer knows how "—discovered that the tenure of the lands and hereditaments of the Hospital had been granted in Franck Almoigne. Such a grant, giving absolute freedom from Royal tax or rent—creating, as it were, an ' imperium in imperio '—he declared to be in its own nature null and void. The conscience of Tyrconnell being fortified by this opinion, and other " specious pretences," he seized, as already seen, the earliest opportunity for giving them effect.

It has not been ascertained that any new Charter was actually issued. " But the said Lord Tyrconnell did manage all things solely by his own will and pleasure." Among other things, he inducted, in December, 1688, an order of Friars to the charge of the Chapel, giving them quarters in the rooms adjoining. This proved " the last straw ' in the case of Robert Curtis, Esq., the Registrar. Apprehending that the Charter and records would at length be taken from him, he fled, as many others did at the time, to England, and, faithful to his trust, brought those treasures with him. " This man," writes the pious Dr Burton,[1] " deserves highly our gratitude, as he was the

[1] Dr. Burton wrote a History of the Royal Hospital about 1843, which contains some interesting matter. He shrewdly suspects Tyrconnell of a desire, at some favourable juncture, to restore the Hospital to the Knights Hospitallers ! He employes 262 words in describing the fireplace of the dining-hall, from which the following " tit-bit " is extracted : " When I approach it, methinks it looks

instrument under God of preserving the immunities of the House to us, the Royal Charter, and the Register books ; he appears to have been raised up for the occasion."

There is now, in addition to the memorandum already mentioned, but little evidence as to the further management, by Tyrconnell, of the affairs of the Royal Hospital during the ensuing year and a half. It is most likely, however, that several persons, of ecclesiastical and other distinction there, left it hurriedly to accompany King James on his journey to Kinsale in July, 1690. And it is certain that after William the Third had passed the Boyne, the sick and wounded men of his army were, by His Majesty's order, as there was wanting a convenient place for their reception, placed in the Royal Hospital. William also ordered Colonel Venner, who had been appointed Master by Tyrconnell, to remain in office during the war.[1] The building was made use of for the reception and treatment of sick and wounded until the close of the Irish Campaign, "the men being maintained out of the soldier's established deductions."

At length, on the 15th November, 1692, a properly constituted Board (consisting of His Excellency, the Lord Lieutenant Sidney, The Lord Chancellor [*not* Fitton],

very awful and knowing, and almost ready to speak, anxious to utter wonders ; there is a grandeur about it I cannot explain—it looks very wise and learned, but bides the time when stones and timber shall thunder forth their secrets : it is of a placid, contented character, and seems satisfied with its position, for my readers must know 'tis not the fire for cooking," etc., etc. He was the assistant Reader (an office now abolished), and subsequently became a Jesuit.

[1] Dr. Burton's sketch of Colonel Venner is as follows : " Never was there a more happy specimen of these rich rags of royalty than Colonel Venner. Methinks I see him now before me stand, shaking his head and side locks in asseveration of the truth of what he witnessed, tapping his gold-mounted tortoise-shell snuff-box, while standing at the south entrance of the Hall, or pulling out his gold turnip-watch, with dian hunt relieved, dogs panting and breathing, or in bushy thickets lost. The inadvertent stroke of a brother veteran's doeskin gauntlet has killed the pet fly that by day perched on his shoulder, and which at night he sheltered beneath a wineglass ; but the dinner drum dispels the cloud gathering upon his brow."

The Lord Archbishop of Dublin, The Earl of Longford, Lord Chief Justice Pyne, Colonel Wolseley, Master of the Ordnance, and Sir Cyril Wyche) was assembled. A number of the wounded soldiers having recovered, the Governors made room for several of the old men that were formerly in the Hospital. "But there remained," says the old Chronicle, "many of the sick and wounded of the army, admitted in the Warr Time. The Governors from time to time, as these Recovered or Dyed, admitted others into the House, that were qualified according to the Charter."

Mrs. Frances Goodwin sent in a new proposal concerning the washing of shirts, sheets, towels, caps, cravats, and also rollers for the wounded, to that august Board which met on 17th November, 1692 ; and Peter, the Providore (who doubtless was some near relative of hers) was also found safe and sound after all the recent disturbances and spilling of blood. The Governors agreed to Mrs. Goodwin's proposal (with some reductions), and gave to Peter a new bill of fare, which is also here set down.

"To be provided every day for each soldiers by the Purveyor, at the rate of 4d. per diem for each man, and £20 per annum for beer.

"Sunday, Monday, Tuesday, Thursday.	One pint of water-gruel for breakfast, one pound of beef or mutton for dinner, one quart of broth for supper, and one pound of bread, and three pints of beer each day.
"Wednesday & Saturday.	Half-a-pound of good cheese, or three pints of peas porridge and butter for each day, one quart of water-gruel, one pound of bread, and three pints of beer.
"Friday.	Fish, a sufficient allowance, according to the season, with butter, as formerly allowed, one quart water-gruel, one pound of bread, and three pints of beer."

CHAPTER VI

EXTRACTS FROM THE RECORDS

FROM the first foundation the management of the Royal Hospital has been singularly free from gross abuses—such as, for instance, are exhibited in the earlier history of Chelsea Hospital. That creditable result has been certainly due to the high status of the Board of Governors, and to the active interest which from the beginning they took in their duties. Some frauds were, it is true, carried on about the earlier part of the 18th century, essentially an age of peculation, but they were not suffered to proceed to a serious extent, nor to impair the efficiency of the institution. In this chapter are collected a series of extracts from the minute books. They will serve to illustrate the administration and interior economy of the Hospital, and that too in the more vivid and impressive manner which belongs to original records.

1693—April 7—Ordered—That each soldier in the Hospital be allowed 2d. every week for buying tobacco.

1697—October 21st—Ordered—that two of the Governors be appointed alternately to visit the Hospital once every week, to inspect all matters relating to the management of the house, and to represent to the Board such miscarriages or disorders as they shall observe.

1700—December 16th—Ordered—That it be an established rule, that if any soldier of the Hospital shall presume to marry, he be immediately turned out of the house, and the Hospital clothes taken from him.[1]

[1] This order has not been suffered to become a dead letter. Eight men were turned out on April 29, 1711, for " marrying contrary to ye rules of ye house." Seven of these were, however, subsequently readmitted as an act of grace. Other instances have occasionally occurred.

1701—December 24th—Ordered—That no work be directed, nor any expense or disbursement charged or paid out of the revenue of the Hospital, without the consent or order of the major part of the Governors first obtained.

1703—September 22nd—The Governors having referred to the Committee the further consideration of the petition of the old and disabled soldiers in the Hospital, containing several matters of complaint, the said petition was read and the particulars thereof inquired into and examined. And as to the complaint of the badness of the diet, and the coarseness of the bread, the Committee are of opinion, so far as yet appears to them, the said soldiers have had no reasonable cause to complain, and do conceive the practice among the said soldiers of selling their provisions is very disorderly, and by no means to be allowed of hereafter. And they are of opinion that Sir Patrick Dunn, Physician of the Hospital, and Mr. Peter Goodwin, the Prodivore, be directed to settle a particular table for more suitable diet for such soldiers, who, by reason of their great age, or other infirmities or distempers, cannot eat the common food, which will obviate all their pretensions for selling their provisions, and prevent it for the future.

1706—December 17th—For the better preservation and attendance of the soldiers *many having been lost for want of a Surgeon being at hand, either to bleed or apply other present remedies*, the Master appointed Robert Curtis Surgeon's Mate, resident Surgeon of the Hospital.

1710—Dec. 11th—The Governors taking into consideration the clothing of the decayed officers, and what particulars will be fit to be provided for them in order to their decent appearing at the Hospital as Commissioned officers, —Resolved—That each officer be furnished with a Scarlet Coat, an Athlone Hat laced with Gold Lace, and a pair of Blue Worsted Stockings, to be paid for out of the pay of each officer.

1712—March 5th—An order from Their Excellencies the Lord Justices, dated the 17th day of January, 1712 (directing the Governors of the Hospital to appoint so

D

much of the Hospital Ground as shall be thought most proper and necessary for erecting two Powder Magazines) being read, and the Governors having considered the said order, and the several clauses, in their Charter relating to their ground, were unanimously of opinion that by the said Charter it was *not in their power* to alienate any of the said ground. [Answer was returned to the Lords Justices accordingly].

1736—Aug. 7th—Ordered—That no more than 180 men, including Sergeants, Corporals, and Drummers, shall be sent to mount guard in town.[1]

1744—March 1st—Mary Storey being recommended to the Board as having served in the Army and an object of compassion,—Ordered—That she be allowed 18d. a week on the Out-pension from this day.[2]

1769—Nov. 29th—It appearing to your Committee, as well as by the information of the Surgeon of the Hospital, and particularly by an instance of this day of the soldiers discharged from the 62nd Foot, that numbers of the soldiers (especially those who come from abroad) are violently afflicted with scorbutic disorders—being advised, we also approving of the same, that Lucan Spa Water may be of great service to them, are therefore of opinion that a car with proper vessels and a horse should be immediately provided and maintained at the Hospital expense for this salutary purpose, and that the Registrar do issue warrants for the same and the charges that may occur thereby.

---

[1] The veterans of the Institution were for many years required to furnish their quota of the city guard.

[2] Two instances of female pensioners occur also on the Chelsea registers. One of these, Catherine Walsh (otherwise Cavanagh), was a native of Dublin. Her career was most extraordinary. She served at first in a regiment of foot, and afterwards in Stair's Dragoons. She was wounded thrice in battle—at Landen in 1693, at Donawert in 1702, and at Ramilies in 1706—and on another occasion by a sergeant of her own regiment in a duel. She also spent nine months as a prisoner in France. The other, Hannah Snell, enlisted in the Guise's Regiment of Foot about 1745, but soon deserted and joined the marines. She served for several years in the East Indies, and was invalided home on account of a severe wound received at Pondicherry.

1794—July 25th—The Master having informed the Board that he had received a notice from the Law Agent of the Corporation of Dublin *claiming a right on the part of the Corporation to fish in the River Liffey opposite the Hospital lands,*—

The Governors were pleased to declare their full determination to support the rights and privileges of the Hospital against the Corporation of the City of Dublin, or any persons whatsoever who may attempt to injure such rights and privileges.

1802—Jan. 12th—Ordered that on Christmas Day, St. Patrick's Day, and the King's Birth Day, each man should receive a double allowance of rations, and two quarts of Ale in lieu of Beer.

.   .   .   .

And for the further comfort of the Soldiers, it was ordered —That they should be provided with Separate Beds, and appropriate Bedding for the same.

.   .   .   .

The Providore having declined continuing his contract for victualling the officers and men, *on account of the high and uncertain prices of provisions,*—

Ordered—That in future the provisions shall be supplied by the Governors advertising in the public papers, &c.

1804—May 1st—Ordered—That the Window Tax, hitherto paid by the officers of the Establishment, shall in future be charged in the Accounts of the Hospital.

June 12th—Ordered—That Joseph Smith, Esq., be appointed Agent for paying the Out-pensioners resident in Great Britain, to prevent the loss sustained by the Pensioners resident there in procuring cash for their bills, and also the loss by exchange.

1805—June 12th—A memorial by the Auditor and Registrar praying that Ralph Smyth, Esq., might be joined in commission with him was submitted.

And the Governors having proceeded to take the same into consideration, and having observed that it has for a long series of years become a practice to permit the appointments to certain offices in the Royal Hospital to be sold, and that the present offices, or most of them, were actually purchased, have resolved :—

That it is the opinion of this Board that the said practice is contrary to the interests of the Institution. That it is the duty of the Governors to take such measures as may be competent to them towards the abolition of this practice, without prejudice to the present holders of the situations. That if Mr. Smyth is joined in commission with Mr. Disney, and should afterwards succeed to office, in the event of the redemption of the office, or of the appointment of a successor by purchase, he will not be considered as having any claim to a higher price than what was paid by Mr. Disney on his appointment, viz. : £3,200.

Which Resolutions having been communicated to Mr. Smyth, the Governors were pleased to approve of his being joined in commission with Mr. Disney.

1808—Aug. 3rd—Ordered—That the Chamberlain make out a return of the hearths in the different officers' apartments, and that the Hearth-Tax for the same be forthwith paid.

1818—Sept. 9th—The Governors were pleased to sign a permission to John Green, Fishmonger, for fishing in the River Liffey opposite the Hospital lands.

1819—April 28th—Ordered—That the Registrar acquaint Mr. Crofton, as a right to visit the Chapel of the Royal Hospital has been claimed by the Coadjutor of the Archbishop of Dublin, which right is doubted by the Governors and is now under discussion, they cannot authorise Mr. Crofton to attend the visitation as Chaplain of this Institution, lest by so doing their rights should be involved.

October 6th—The Board considering that no right has been proved on the part of the Archbishop of Dublin to visit their Chapel,—Ordered—That the Chaplain be instructed not to admit the Rural Dean in future to visit the Chapel.

1821—July 14th—The Board having taken into consideration the claim of the Archbishop of Dublin to visit the Chapel of this Institution, is of opinion that the Chapel of Kilmainham Hospital, being a Royal Chapel, is exempt from the jurisdiction of the Archbishop of Dublin, and is not visitable by His Grace's Rural Dean.

1824—May 26th—Ordered—That the soldiers of Kilmainham Hospital be furnished with a pair of Mits and a pair of Gaiters once in two years, as it appears that the soldiers of Chelsea Hospital are provided with those articles.

December 29th—That one quart of the best table beer per diem be issued to each soldier in the Hospital in future, instead of two quarts per diem of the quality heretofore supplied.

1846—September 28th—Resolved that the Governors approve of the Richmond Tower being removed (from the foot of Watling Street) and rebuilt at the entrance to the Hospital by the Western Avenue,—and it is ordered that the Great Southern and Western Railway Company be informed accordingly, in reply to Mr. Taylor's letter of the 22nd July last (offering to have this work done at the expense of the Company, as the Tower was an obstruction to traffic between the city and Kingsbridge station).

1847—June 28th—The Deputy-Master having informed the Governors that Sir William Betham, Ulster King-at-Arms, had promised to give Armorial Bearings for this Institution—Ordered—That the Registrar do request him to furnish them at his early convenience, with a view to having the same placed on the Tower, now erecting at the Western Entrance.

CHAPTER VII

MODERN HISTORY OF THE HOSPITAL

THE ROYAL HOSPITAL continued its useful work unruffled by untoward occurrences until 1916, when the rebellion of that year drew it into the troublous events which then distracted Ireland. The hospital became a strong point and was occupied by 2,500 troops of various regiments, every available space being utilised to accommodate the soldiers. The executive command devolved on Brigadier-General Maconchy.

Although the House was not actually attacked it was more or less continuously under rebel fire. A special guard was detailed for the defence of the House itself, and this guard took an active part in repressing the rebellion.

The rebels had taken up their position in the Malt House, Bow Lane, but their fire was silenced by two machine-gun sections which had been placed on the roof of the building which is now the residence of the Chief General Staff Officer of the Command.

At one time the rations of the garrison ran short, and for several days the In-pensioners, like everyone else, found themselves on the Active Service diet of bully-beef and biscuits.

Nine N.C.O's and men of the Army killed during that period are buried in Bully's Acre, and within the Board Room of the Hospital is filed a complete list of all the Officers, N.C.O's, and men who lost their lives during the rebellion.

After the rebellion a short-lived peace descended on the Hospital, but was disturbed early in 1920, when the Sinn Fein struggles again cast gloom and terror over the land,

Investiture held on July 12, 1921, by General the Rt. Hon. Sir Nevil Macready, the Master.

[Facing page 54.

and its defence in case of attack had again to be seriously considered. It was then used to house many of the officers working at the General Headquarters of the Command who took up their residence there.

The Hospital has from time to time been used as a temporary vice-regal residence—Lord French, the hero of Mons and Yprés, stayed there previous to taking up his residence at the Vice-Regal Lodge, and it was within its ancient walls that he bade farewell to the Officers of General Headquarters and to the Pensioners on the 29th April, 1921, the 241st anniversary of the day that the foundation stone of the hospital was laid.

On the 12th July, 1921, the Commander-in-Chief, General Sir Nevil Macready, held an investiture within the main court-yard, when soldiers who had distinguished themselves by especial acts of gallantry in the field received decorations.

It is of interest to note that a superstition hangs about the place to the effect that if the rooks which build in the main avenue leave it, fortune, for a time, leaves the Hospital. About 1916 the rooks took their departure, and only returned in 1921, a year the close of which saw all eyes fixed on Ireland and all hearts hoping that the long years of unhappiness would end in tranquillity and contentment.

May peace come to abide in Ireland, and may its advent see this ancient and historic Institution as firmly established to carry out its humane duties as it has been now for nearly 250 years.

PART II

CHAPTER VIII

GOVERNMENT OF THE HOSPITAL

As originally constituted by the Charter of Charles the Second, the Board of Governors, in whom was invested the supreme management of the affairs of the Hospital, consisted of all the principal civil, military, and ecclesiastical personages in Ireland, beginning with the Lord Lieutenant. But much difficulty was experienced in getting together a *major* part of the Governors, as required by that Charter, for the lawful transaction of business. In consequence, a fresh Charter was granted by King George the Second, in 1758, which fixed a legal quorum at seven.

The present constitution of the Board (a few of the original offices having become void, and others of a similar nature having been substituted, as provided for in Charles, Charter), is as follows :

Civil

1. His Excellency the Lord Lieutenant.
2.[1] His Grace The Lord Primate of all Ireland.
3. His Grace The Lord Archbishop of Dublin.
4.[1] Right Hon. The Lord Chancellor of Ireland.
5. Right Hon. The Lord Chief Justice of Ireland.
6. Right Hon. The Chief Secretary for Ireland.

Military

1. General Officer Commanding the Forces in Ireland.
2. Major-General Commanding Dublin District.
3. Principal Medical Officer in Ireland.

[1] These offices were held conjointly in 1684.

4.[1] Deputy Adjutant General.
5.[1] Deputy Quartermaster General.
6. Chief Engineer in Ireland.
7. Commandant Royal Hibernian Military School.
8. Assistant Director of Ordnance Services.
9. Assistant Military Secretary.

The general superintendence and control of the whole establishment is assigned by Royal Warrant to the General Commanding the Forces in Ireland, as Master. He is aided by his Deputy Adjutant General as Deputy Master, and the following staff of officers :

A. The Commandant and Secretary.
B. The Physician and Surgeon.

There is also a Quartermaster-Sergeant, and a staff of eight nurses. A number of minor offices are filled from among the In-pensioners, who thus obtain an addition, as extra-duty pay, to their money allowances. The posts thus available are :—Chapel Clerk, Armourer, Lodge-Keeper, Infirmary Sergeant, Infirmary Orderly, Cooks and Assistants, Messenger to Board-Room, Hall Keeper, Barber, Coal Porters, etc. Some few men of more robust constitution are occasionally admitted for such of these appointments as require superior health and strength.

A list of the Masters since its foundation will be found in Appendix VII. It includes the names of Sir Ralph Abercrombie, General Lake, Lord Combermere, Lord Roberts, Lord Wolseley, the Duke of Connaught, and others distinguished in the military annals of their country, the office having been vested in the General Commanding the Forces in Ireland since the year 1775.

---

[1] In whom the duties of Major-General i/c Administration are temporarily vested.

CHAPTER IX

THE PENSION ESTABLISHMENTS

REFERENCE has already been made to some old men, who were turned out of the army, having been pensioned on half-pay from the Hospital revenue. This system gradually developed, in spite of persistent effort to meet all requirements by increasing the In-pension establishment. In August, 1697, it was ordered "That no superannuated officer or soldier of the Hospital be allowed to lodge out of the House, or to have money instead of diet." But in the following April the Governors appear to have altered their views ; and they formally sanctioned a rate of 18d. a week, without clothes, for "such old and disabled soldiers as shall be viewed and approved of, instead of their maintenance in the Hospital." Out-pensioners under this scheme were allowed to remove into the country, but were required to attend a general muster at the end of every three months.

A wider interpretation was also given to the terms of the Charter, which could not fail to increase the number of applicants. It was resolved (18 Feb., 1699) "That any soldier who has served His Majesty in *England, Ireland,* Flanders, or other foreign parts for *seven years*, and belongs to any regiment now on the *Irish* establishment, or who served in any regiment formerly on the said establishment, is qualified for the Hospital."

In the same year (1699) it was agreed to raise the number to be provided for, in the Hospital, to 400 ; and to include among these the 33 soldiers who were at the time upon Out-pension. In 1701, "there being 41 soldiers allowed 18d. per week each until they can be otherwise provided

for," it was ordered that they should be admitted into
the Hospital, towards making up the number of 450,
" as soon as bedding, clothing, and other necessaries can
be provided for them." This was the greatest number
ever accommodated in the Hospital. It would appear
that some temporary buildings were added at that time
to the House. (An interesting document showing the
annual revenue and expenditure of the period is printed
as Appendix VIII.) Shortly afterwards, however, 31
soldiers were allowed at their own request to revert to the
Out-pension list on 18d. a week. The number of In-pensioners thus reduced to 419 was again increased in March,
1704, and fixed at 425, as the Governors found that the
revenue was affording an annual surplus. But the funds
were by no means adequate to the pension wants of the
army in Ireland. In this connection a sombre record
of the year 1711 must not be passed over. It exhibits
His Excellency Lord Justice Ingoldsby representing to
the Governors " that there are several disabled soldiers
lately discharged out of the army in a starving condition,
who have petitioned for the relief of the Hospital, but
cannot be admitted for want of vacancies." In consequence of the Lord Justice's humane intervention the
Governors added 5 men to the 425 already maintained
in the House.

Meantime the Out-pension list was steadily increasing.
An order which was issued in 1715 provided that any one
upon that list who should be discovered to beg would,
upon conviction, be struck off it. But after a time only
the small pittance of 12d. a week could be afforded to the
majority of those affected by this order, and it will be
readily supposed that begging, in some instances, must
have been a necessary supplement.

While matters were thus circumstanced, and the revenue
of the Hospital employed to the utmost, a letter from His
Majesty's Secretary at War to the Lords Justices was
passed on to the Governors (Feb., 1716), and created
considerable discussion and consternation among them.

It signified His Majesty's pleasure that 60 invalid soldiers, *who had been found qualified by the Commissioners at the Horse Guards*, should be placed upon the pension of the Royal Hospital, near Dublin. The Governors stated that under the charter they had *no power* to comply with this request, as those soldiers had not served for seven years, nor been maimed in the army of Ireland. Their plea was accepted ; and subsequently, in 1726, the King made a grant to them of £1,183 per annum in aid of the Out-pension fund. With this assistance the number of Out-pensioners was augmented from 413 to 570, and the rate of pension from 12d. to 18d. a week—(13 only of the former number having been in receipt of the 18d.).

In 1729 there were 30 men reduced from the House to the Out-pension, with a view to the support of a greater number of Out-pensioners. By this means the number in the House was left at 400, and for 54 years no serious variation was made as regards the number pensioned on either system.

In 1783, after the cessation of the War of Independence in America, the number of sergeants on the Out-pension was increased from 20 to 100 ; of corporals, from 16 to 100 ; sergeants on the In-pension from 8 to 12 ; corporals from 6 to 10; and upon an address from the Irish House of Commons to the King in 1785, £4,000 was granted to the Governors of the Hospital to enable them to carry into effect the following plan of Out-pensions :

20 Sergeant-Majors at £18 5s. each a year	... 1s. per day.			
100 Sergeants	,, £10 os.	,,		
100 Corporals	,, £8 os.	,,		
500 Soldiers	,, £7 12s. 1d.	,,	... 5d.	,,
1,200 Soldiers	,, £6 1s. 8d.	,,	... 4d.	,,
570 Soldiers	,, £4 11s. 3d.	,,	... 3d.	,,

Thus in all about 2,500 Out-pensioners, and 400 In-pensioners were provided for.

The following special order, dated 31st July, 1802, affords some token, when the rates of pension are compared with those last set down, of the gratification with which the achievements of the British land forces against the French in Egypt were contemplated : " That all the sergeants that shall be admitted pensioners, who are blind from service in Egypt, shall be paid a pension of 1s. 6d. per day ; all corporals, 1s. 2d. ; and drummers and privates 1s. per day."

In 1804 privates discharged from the 4th Garrison Battalion (which was then quartered in Ireland and composed of old soldiers), who were unfit for further military service, were allowed a pension of 9d. a day, or, if totally incapacitated by infirmity, of 1s. a day. This provision, and others previously treated of, merely assimilated from time to time the Irish scale of Out-pension to that awarded by the Commissioners of Chelsea Hospital. Evidently it would have been unfair to adopt different rates, the only ground of distinction being that of service in Ireland.

The 6d. poundage rate on the pay of the Army in Ireland, by means of which Kilmainham Hospital had been originally established and supported, ceased by order of the Government to be deducted in 1794. In lieu thereof, Parliamentary grants have been annually voted since that date—the financial control of the Hospital thus coming into the hands of the War Minister.

At the end of 1806 the Act of Parliament regarding soldiers' pensions, known as Mr. Windham's, came into force. By it their claims were definitely established and determined, and rates authoritatively fixed according to length and nature of service. The soldier could now demand a pension as a legal right, and was entitled to a much higher rate than heretofore. This statute was, however, repealed in 1826, and pensions again made *technically* dependent on *the bounty of the Crown*. But practically the advantages conferred by it have since been continued ; and the scale of pension has been gradually, if slowly, raised according as the nation's sense of duty or necessity in this respect has become quickened.[1]

[1] It was not until 1874 that any special provision was made for the surviving heroes of the immortal victory of 1815. Under happier auspices, special pensions are now being awarded to those who served in the Crimean, Indian Mutiny, and other campaigns before 1860.

One important effect of increasing the rate of Out-pension has been a diminution in the number of applicants for admission to the Royal Hospitals at Chelsea and Kilmainham. This, of course, is well, considering how limited is the demand which could be met in that way. So long as men are able to make an addition to their pensions by labour they prefer to remain with their friends and to retain the command of their own money. But for those who have no relatives, or whose last years must be spent in dependence on others, the Hospital affords a suitable and necessary refuge.

An attempt was made in the year 1834 to do away with the In-pension establishment of Kilmainham altogether. The Out-pensioners had twelve years previously been by Act of Parliament transferred to the control of the Chelsea Commissioners.[1] It was conceived that Chelsea Hospital might also be sufficient for the whole Army as regards the special wants which render In-pensions an advantage. It was forgotten that Kilmainham Hospital met the wants of the Irish soldier in his own country, that in this connection it had secured a place in the affections of the Irish people, and more particularly of the citizens of Dublin. But the grounds and building had attracted the attention of the Ordnance Department as affording accommodation which might suit the Artillery better than the inferior and unhealthy quarters at that time available in Island Bridge Barracks. Careful calculation showed that it would be cheaper to fit up Kilmainham Hospital for the Artillery and to turn out the old men on tempting pensions, or bring those who were willing over to Chelsea Hospital, than to renovate the Barracks at Island Bridge.

Lieut.-General Sir Hussey Vivian was at that time in command of the forces in Ireland. Almost alone in official circles he opposed the arbitrary design.[2] But he was a

[1] There were 15,379 Out-pensioners of Kilmainham Hospital at the time of transfer, December, 1822.

[2] He was strongly supported, however, by the Board of Governors of the Hospital.

distinguished officer who on the eventful day of Waterloo had commanded a brigade with glory and success, and was not one to give up his case in a careless manner. His repeated remonstrances, backed by a petition from the citizens of Dublin and the nobility and gentry of Ireland, proved successful. Much gratification was felt at this result ; likewise much irritation at the persistent efforts at spoliation which had been made. Some few years afterwards Mr. (subsequently Chief Justice) Whiteside, in expressing popular feeling on the business, said: "They read not very long since a debate got up by the economists as to the prudence of removing the broken-down Irish pensioners from Kilmainham to Chelsea, to effect a little saving, careless of the feelings, the associations, the joys or the griefs of the poor old Irish soldiers who had bravely served their country. That cruelty was prevented by something like an exhibition of national spirit and national indignation."

Admissions to the Hospital had been stopped while its fate was pending. In 1838 it was re-opened and the establishment of In-pensioners fixed at 200. This figure was further reduced to 140, the present number, by Royal Warrant in 1854.

A second attempt to abolish Kilmainham In-pension was made in 1853. This was opposed by Isaac Butt. He obtained an order of the House of Commons to have the correspondence which took place between Sir Hussey Vivian and the other authorities in 1834 printed and laid before the House. The motion of abolition then fell through. The Committees which have since reported to Parliament upon the affairs of the Hospital have not recommended any serious change in its management nor any withdrawal of that special provision which the nation has made at Kilmainham for deserving Irish soldiers.[1] In the words of the late Lord Sandhurst : " Although it would be impossible to house all the Out-pensioners of a large army, never-

[1] There are seldom as many as twelve In-pensioners of Kilmainham who are not of Irish nationality.

theless it does appear to me very advantageous to have such an institution as Kilmainham in the capital of Ireland, which may be the resort of a few old worn-out soldiers, or of men who have lost their limbs in the service of their country. I believe the moral and political good performed by such institutions far to exceed the physical comfort bestowed by them on a few individuals."

There are two branches of the activity of the Royal Hospital which have fallen into abeyance. There was formerly a Widows' House in which the relict of a Soldier was supported, and for the maintenance of which £100 a year was allowed. Formerly, also, there were six Captains of Invalids, Officers on the Retired List, whose services and financial position rendered them fit objects for the hospitality of the Hospital These Officers were wont to live upon the first floor of the Hospital, and arrangements were made for their feeding and comfort in a style suitable to their rank. As time went on their numbers were reduced first to four, and finally there remained only one.

Time came when, in 1891, this Officer's quarters were required for other military purposes, and he was granted an annuity of £120 and left the Hospital.

CHAPTER X

IN-PENSIONERS

THE number of Pensioners now provided for in Kilmainham Hospital is 140. A few of these are admitted for the performance of special duty, but the remainder are selected purely on the grounds of age, service, and infirmity.

The several ranks, with their money allowances, were fixed by Royal Warrant dated 1854 as follows:

1 Sergeant-Major	at 2/6 a day.	
6 Company Sergeants	,, 8d.	,,
6 Corporals	,, 4d.	,,
4 Drummers	,, 3d.	,,
10 Privates, 1st class	,, 2d.	,,
20 ,, 2nd ,,	,, 1½d.	,,
93 ,, 3rd ,,	,, 1d.	,,

The above ranks and allowances have been amended from time to time through the introduction of New Royal Warrants or financial decisions of the Treasury; this occurred in 1907 and 1913, and again in 1920.

The following show the several ranks with their money allowances per diem as they exist at the present time:

1 Sergeant-Major at,	from	2/6 to 3/-
1 Quartermaster Sergeant	,,	2/- ,, 2/6
1 Infirmary Sergeant	,,	2/- ,, 2/6
1 Master Cook	,,	2/- ,, 2/6
6 Company Sergeants at	,,	1/-
6 Corporals	,,	6d.
4 Drummers	,,	4½d.
10 Privates	,,	4d.
20 ,,	,,	3½d.
91 ,,	,,	3d.

E

The maximum rate in the case of each of the first four officials is attained after three years' service in his appointment. Those who hold special appointments receive extra duty pay at different rates, ranging from 6d. to 1s. a day : on an average about 24 are constantly employed in these special duties.

All In-pensioners are fed, clothed, and lodged, receive medical attendance and care, and have every convenience for religious worship, reading, and those light relaxations which pass the time for the aged and feeble.

Their dietary allowance is, for each man : 8 ozs. bacon, Tuesday and Saturday, ¾lb. beef or mutton, Sunday, Monday, Wednesday, Thursday, and Friday (meat being issued without bone) ; 16 ozs. bread, 4 ozs. flour, ½ oz. tea, 8 ozs. vegetables, 1 oz. butter, 2 ozs. sugar, 1 pint porter or ½ oz. tobacco in lieu, ¾ pint milk, 16 ozs. potatoes each day ; also 1¼ oz. oatmeal or barley on Sunday, Thursday, and Friday.

An allowance of ¾d. per man per day (now increased to 1¼d. as a temporary measure) is allowed for the purpose of supplying an extra for the tea meal.

The west end of the great hall is set aside for the old men as a dining hall and recreation room ; this they much prefer to the old custom of having to carry their dinners in mess tins to their own rooms.

Breakfast is served at 8 a.m. ; dinner at 12.45. p.m. ; tea at 5 p.m.

After each meal the old men may be seen moving to their several rooms, or, for a morning walk, to the beautiful avenue of the Hospital, while in the afternoon, more likely, they take a siesta.

They live together in rooms each of which accommodates from four to six ; this arrangement was highly approved by a Parliamentary Committee in 1870 as conducing more to domestic comfort than the more solitary system of Chelsea Hospital, where each man has a separate, but small, compartment. Full particulars of the furniture of the rooms are contained in the report of that Committee, and students of domestic economy are referred to it. Cleanliness and neatness and military order are everywhere present.

Into the details of the carefully arranged system of the supply of clothing it is not necessary to enter. The blue coat, the red coat, the blue jacket and forage cap are familiar through all the western part of the city. Cocked hats, such as we must suppose Corporal Trim and Uncle Toby to have worn at Blenheim, are donned on special occasions.

The qualifications for admission to the Hospital are set out in the official statement furnished to Pensioners as follows :

1. Inability to add to out-pensions by labour or other industry.

2. Attainment to the age of 55 years in the case of soldiers of full service.

3. Present suffering from a disability, clearly caused by army service, in the case of a soldier who has not served his full time.

4. Freedom from responsibility for the support of wife or child.

5. Good character while in the service, and since discharge.

Temporary Pensioners are not eligible. Application for admission should be made to the Secretary. From the list of applicants, under these conditions, the Board of the Hospital, which meets once a month, makes selections as vacancies arise. Some notion of the stamp of men thus selected may be gathered from the fact that 75 of the present inmates are in possession of War Medals to the number of 111. (For detail, see Appendix VI.) A brief summary of the services, etc., of a few men will not be out of place here.

At Present in the Hospital

Among the In-pensioners who have seen war service there are certain veterans whose experiences entitle them to especial attention on account of the far-off days and varying scenes of which they are the survivors.

In-pensioners J. McGrath and A. McCormick, late of the Royal Irish Regiment and Welsh Regiment respectively, served in the Crimea in 1854. The former wears, in addition to the British and Turkish medals, the clasp for Sebastopol. In-pensioner J. King, late of the 87th Foot, now the Royal Irish Fusiliers, was in the Indian Mutiny and wears the clasp for Lucknow.

In-pensioner P. Carty, late 67th Foot, survives the China War of 1860. In-pensioners P. Gaffney and W. Cox, late of the 60th Rifles and 47th Foot respectively, served during the Reill Rebellion of 1860 in Canada. J. Scotton, late Yorkshire Regiment, saw service in Hazara in 1868, and there are two men who fought against the Maoris in New Zealand in 1866, Sergeant J. Tuck, late 43rd Light Infantry, and In-pensioner J. Smith, late of the Royal Irish Regiment.

Their ages seem to bring us in touch with the gallant deeds of more than two generations ago. McCormick and King are now 86, McGrath is 85, while Smith is 83.

Former Inmates

Christopher E. Hanlon, 13th Hussars. Pension 11d. Service 24 years ; Crimea, 2 years ; and Canada 2$\frac{10}{12}$ years. Discharged in August, 1861. Character "very good." (Three good conduct badges) Died in the Hospital on 15th February, 1890, aged 63.

Served in Crimean war. Present at Balaclava and Sebastopol. *Was engaged in the charge of the Light Brigade ; severely wounded in the neck by a lance, and taken prisoner of war ; had a horse shot under him and rifle bullet passed through his clothing across his breast and passed out through his bridle arm.*

Had Crimean and Turkish medals with 2 clasps ; and good conduct medal.

Joseph Binns, Royal Sappers and Miners. Pension 4½d. Service of 6 years, of which 5 were spent in the Peninsula. Discharged in 1817 with a " good " character. Admitted to the Hospital in July, 1878, AND DIED THERE ON 24TH JANUARY, 1881, at the age of 84.

Served in Peninsular war. Present at blockade of Pampeluna, siege and storming of S. Sebastian, and blockade of Bayonne. Was wounded on 31st August, 1813, at San Sebastian, in shoulder and right thigh.

Received Peninsular medal.

———

John Cosgrove, 39th Regiment. Pension 6d. Total service 18$\frac{180}{365}$ years ; in Peninsula and France 8 years ; North America 1 year ; discharged in June, 1825. Character "good." Admitted to the Hospital in April, 1854, and died there on 7th November, 1875, aged 85.

Served in Peninsular war. Present at the battles of Albuhera, Vittoria, Pyrenees, Nivelle, Nive, Orthes, and Toulouse, and Platsburgh.

Peninsular medal and 5 clasps.

———

Richard Hughes, 1st Regiment. Pension 9d. Total service 10$\frac{6}{12}$ years (including 2 years for Waterloo). Discharged March, 1816. Character "good." Admitted to the Hospital in July, 1854, where he died 10th December, 1877, aged 84.

Served in Peninsular war. Present at Vittoria, S. Sebastian. *Engaged at Waterloo, wounded in right thigh.*

———

Charles Hall, 32nd Foot. Pension 9d. Service 15 years. Served 3 months in Portugal, 9$\frac{6}{12}$ years in Spain, 1 year in Ionian Islands, and 2 years in France. Discharged 19th November, 1827, with " good " character. Was admitted to the Hospital on 1st September, 1873, and died there on *4th December*, 1878, aged 85.

Served in Peninsular war. Was present at battles of *Waterloo* and Cayal ; wounded in the scalp at Waterloo.

Thomas Freeman,[1] 52nd Regiment. Pension 5d. Served 14 years ; all the time at Denmark, and in the Peninsula. Discharged 3rd May, 1820. Character "good." Admitted to the Hospital in April, 1856, and died there on 11th December, 1859, at the age of 70.

Served at the siege of Copenhagen ; afterwards in the Peninsular war, being present at Busaco, Fuentes d'Onor, Ciudad Rodrigo, Badajoz, Salamancà, Vittoria, Nivelle, Nive, Orthes, and Toulouse. Also engaged at *Waterloo*.

Robert Freeman,[1] 52nd Foot. Pension 1s. Service 14 years, 9 of which were spent in Denmark, Spain, and Portugal. Discharged 22nd March, 1820, with an "excellent" character. Admitted to the Hospital on 1st November, 1859, and died there on 20th January, 1860, at the age of 73.

Served in Denmark at the siege of Copenhagen ; afterwards in the Peninsula, where he was present at Vimiera, Busaco, Fuentes d'Onor, Ciudad Rodrigo, Badajoz, Salamanca, Vittoria, Pyrenees, Nivelle, Nive, Orthes, Toulouse. Also present at *Waterloo*, where he was wounded in the head.

James Graham, 12th Dragoons and 2nd Fusilier Guards Pension 9d. Total Service $19\frac{10}{12}$ years (including 2 years boon service for Waterloo). Discharged 13th January, 1730, with "a very good" character. Admitted to the Hospital, 1st July, 1841, and died there on 23rd April, 1845, aged 54.

Present at the battle of Waterloo, and distinguished himself by his gallant conduct in the defence of Hougomont.

[1] These two men were brothers.

He is referred to in Siborne's history of the campaign of 1815, as follows :—"The French, however, succeeded in forcing the gate [of Hougomont] ; but the defenders betook themselves to the nearest cover, whence they poured a fire upon the intruders, and then rushing forward a struggle ensued which was distinguished by the most intrepid courage on both sides. At length Lieut.-Colonel MacDonell, Captain Wyndham, Ensigns Gooch and Hervey, and Sergeant Graham, of the Coldstream Guards, by dint of personal strength and exertions, combined with extraordinary bravery and perseverance, succeeded in closing the gate against their assailants.

"This individual" (*i.e.* Sergt. Graham), "deserves honourable mention, having greatly distinguished himself during the memorable defence of Hougomont. At a later period of the day, when in the ranks along the garden wall facing the wood, and when the struggle was most severe in that quarter, he asked Lieut.-Colonel McDonell's permission to fall out. The Colonel, knowing the character of the man, expressed his surprise at the request made at such a moment. Graham explained that his brother lay wounded in one of the buildings then on fire, that he wished to remove him to a place of safety, and that he would then lose no time in rejoining the ranks. The request was granted : Graham succeeded in snatching his brother from the horrible fate which menaced him, laid him in a ditch in rear of the inclosures, and, true to his word, was again at his post.

"Early in August of that year, and while the Anglo-allied army was at Paris, the Duke of Wellington received a letter from the Rev. Mr. Norcross, rector of Framlingham, in Suffolk, expressing his wish to confer a pension of £10 a year, for life, on some Waterloo soldier to be named by his Grace. The Duke requested Sir John Byng (now Lord Stafford) to choose a man from the 2nd brigade of Guards, which had so highly distinguished itself in the defence of Hougomont. Out of numerous instances of good conduct evinced by several individuals of each battalion, Sergeant

James Graham, of the light company of the Coldstream, was selected to receive the proffered annuity, as notified in brigade orders of the 9th of August, 1815. This was paid to him during two years, at the expiration of which period it ceased, in consequence of the bankruptcy of the benevolent donor."

APPENDIX I

AN ACCOUNT OF COST OF BUILDING

	£	s.	d.
To labourers for digging foundations, cellars, etc.	509	12	5¾
To day labourers	557	17	10½
To masons and bricklayers	5,423	7	4½
To stonecutters	1,248	11	7¼
To carpenters	1,639	2	4½
To sawyers	377	17	11¼
To joiners and carvers	809	12	1
To plasterers and painters	1,926	1	1½
To smiths and ironmongers	822	19	3¾
To plumbers	1,081	4	10½
To slaters	801	18	0
To glaziers	319	12	3½
To turners	5	18	9
To paviors	15	13	7½
To tilemakers for tiles	156	8	7½
For timber, deals and laths	5,363	8	5¼
For Portland stones and other hewing stones	1,150	13	0¾
For carriage and freight of timber stone, lead, etc.	371	12	1
For tools, instruments and other contingencies	129	16	3
To overseers and other officers for their salaries	810	0	0
For an engine to raise water for the wash-house	37	18	9

£23,559 16 11¼

APPENDIX II

PAINTINGS IN THE GREAT HALL

ALONG WEST WALL

Thomas Earl of Ossory, Lord Deputy in 1664.
Richard, Earl of Arran, Lord Deputy in 1684.
Sir Cyril Wyche, a Lord Justice in 1696.
King Charles the Second, founder of this Hospital.[1]
Charles, Earl of Berkeley, a Lord Justice in 1699.
Thomas Keightly, Esq., a Lord Justice in 1702.
Sir Richard Cox, Lord Chancellor, a Lord Justice in 1706.

[1] Purchased by the Board in 1700.

King William the Third.[1]
Queen Mary.[1]
Lionel, Duke of Dorset, Lord Lieutenant in 1734.
William, Duke of Devonshire, Lord Lieutenant in 1737.
Queen Anne.[2]
Prince George of Denmark.

Sir Charles Porter, Lord Chancellor, a Lord Justice in 1696.
Michael Boyle, Lord Primate, a Lord Justice in 1685.
Narcissus Marsh, Lord Primate, a Lord Justice in 1699.
Lieut.-General Frederick Hamilton, one of the Governors of this
  Hospital, 1718.

General Thomas Erle, a Lord Justice in 1702.
Lawrence, Earl of Roche, Lord Lieutenant in 1701.
James, Duke of Ormond, Lord Lieutenant in 1662.
Thomas, Lord Coningsby, a Lord Justice in 1690.
Henry, Earl of Galway, a Lord Justice in 1697.

Over the south doorway hangs a portrait of John Henderson, a
former in-pensioner, who lived to the great age of one hundred and
six years (died May 30, 1856).

APPENDIX III

FLAGS AND REGIMENTAL COLOURS IN THE GREAT HALL
AND CHAPEL

In the Great Hall, proceeding by the left from the south door :

  1 Chinese flag (small).

  2. Pole and fragment of colours.
  3. Chinese flag (small).
  4. King's colour, used as a saluting flag in Dublin Castle (early
nineteenth century).
  5. Chinese flag (small).
  6. Pole and fragment of colours.

  7. Chinese flag.
  8. Chinese flag.
  9. Union Jack, colour.

[1] Purchased by the Board in 1700.
[2] Purchased by the Board for £16 during her reign.

10. Union Jack, Queen's colour.
11. Trumpet banner.
12. Militia flag, 3rd Royal Bucks (King's Own).
13. Chinese flag (small).
14. Militia flag, 1st Western Regiment (Northumberland).
15. Trumpet banner.
16. Militia flag, Whitehaven.
17. Militia flag, Archerfield.
18. Pole and fragment of colours.
19. Chinese flag (small).

ON THE EAST WALL

20. Sikh flag, captured during the Punjab Campaign.
21. Guidon and belt, 7th Dragoon Guards (Princess Royal's).
22. Queen's colour, used as a saluting flag in Dublin Castle (middle nineteenth century).
23. Sepoy flag.

REMAINDER OF SOUTH WALL

24. Chinese flag (small).
25. Chinese flag (large).

NOTE.—Numbers 2, 6 and 18 have not been separately identified, though historically the most interesting of the collection. They are relics of the colours carried by the 90th Light Infantry in Egypt under Sir Ralph Abercrombie, 1800-1 (perhaps Nos. 2 and 6) ; and of the colours carried by the 56th Regiment during the siege of Gibraltar, 1779-82 (perhaps No. 18). The standard carried by the Inniskilling Dragoons at the battle of the Boyne, 1690, is in a glass case in the alcove immediately to the right of the main entrance.

In the Chapel, proceeding by the left from the main door :

ON THE NORTH WALL

1. 32nd Regiment (Cornwall), Queen's colour.
2. 32nd Regiment (Cornwall), Regimental colour.
3. 63rd Regiment (Suffolk), Regimental colour.
4. 63rd Regiment (Suffolk), Queen's colour.
5. 15th Regiment (E. Yorkshire), Regimental colour.
6. 15th Regiment (E. Yorkshire), Queen's colour.

ON THE SOUTH WALL

7. Wicklow Militia, Queen's colour.
8. Wicklow Militia, Regimental colour.
9. 30th Regiment (Cambridgeshire), Queen's colour.
10. 30th Regiment (Cambridgeshire), Regimental colour.
11. 59th Regiment, Regimental colour.
12. 59th Regiment, Queen's colour.

NOTE.—The colours of the 1st Royal Regiment, the 7th Royal Fusiliers and the 70th Regiment (Surrey), which formerly hung in the chapel, have been handed over for safe custody to these regiments ; their places are being taken by colours of the Royal Munster Fusiliers and the Connaught Rangers, which are being entrusted to the safe custody of the Governors.

APPENDIX IV

ARMS AND ARMOUR IN THE GREAT HALL

A considerable quantity of the arms and armour specified in the following catalogue was brought from the Tower of London about the year 1829 to the Pigeon House Fort, on the formation of the Armoury at the latter place. In 1891 it was transferred to the Royal Hospital, after being exhibited during the Royal Irish Military Tournament of that year at Ballsbridge.

The visitor is supposed to enter the Great Hall from the Quadrangle, and to commence its circuit by the left hand. A sufficient number of articles may be identified when passing round to give an accurate notion of the entire collection, the large number of specimens of a similar kind—such as helmets, skull-caps, French painted armour, breast-plates, etc.—forbidding a detailed enumeration. Muskets, carbines, and rifles are arranged along the wall in chronological succession, so that the various forms of development up to the Magazine Rifle of 1890 may be readily followed. A separate list of the models of ordnance appears at the end.

1. Suit of black armour with closed helmet, 16th century.

2. Maltese armour, 16th century, black.

3. Armed figure ; bright armour, 17th century, with halberd.

4.   Do.   do.   with cross-handled sword.

5. Armed figure ; bright armour, 17th century, with lance.

6.   Do.   do.   do.   with cross-handled sword.

7. Armed figure ; bright armour, 17th century, with cross-handled sword.

8. Maltese armour, 17th century ; black.

9.   do.   do.

10. Maltese armour, 16th century ; black.

11. Black armour with barred helmet ; Arquebusier, 17th century.

12. Maltese armour, 16th century ; black.

13. Suit of black armour with closed helmet, 17th century.

14. Jousting or tilting spear, 16th century (time of Henry VIII.)

15.   Do.   do.

16. Musket, match-lock, year 1603.

17.   Do.   do.

18. Musket, flint-lock, 1665.

19.   Do.   1688.

20. Swords, heavy cavalry, early 19th century ; arranged in star.

21. Swords, infantry sergeants and yeomen, early 19th century.

22. Scimitars, light cavalry, early 19th century.

23. Swords, mounted service, 1853.

24. Two Bandoliers, ancient, with cartridge pockets.

25. Two skull-caps ; Cromwellian (Roundheads).

26. Breast-plates ; British, early 18th century.

27. (On stand.) Muskets converted from flint-lock to percussion about 1840, with bayonets.

      (There are seven other similar stands in the Hall.)

28. Sergeants' halberds, early 19th century (four).

29. Musket, flint-lock, 1690.
30. Do. do. 1695.
31. Carbine, do. 1690.
32. Musket, do: 1695.
33. Maltese helmets.
34. French painted breast-plates.
35. British backplates, 17th and 18th centuries.
36. Pistol, flint-lock, 1688.
37. Helmet, 3rd Dragoon Guards, modern.
38. Skull-caps, open, Carabineers (ancient).
39. Maltese helmets, 16th century (time of Elizabeth).
40. Life Guards' cuirass, with sword (modern).
41. Swords, cavalry, 1680.
42. Damascus swords, ancient (two).
43. Swords, light cavalry, 4th Hussars (modern).
44. British armour breast-plate, 17th century (Cromwellian).
45. Do. officer's helmet do.
46. Do. trooper's helmet do.
47. Do. musketeer's helmet do.
48. French painted breast-plate.
49. Spanish helmet, 1588. Probably belonged to an officer of high rank. Curiously graven with arms.
50. Boarding pike and scabbard.
51. Helmet used in tilting, late 15th century (time of Henry VII.).
52. French cuirassiers' breast-plate (time of Waterloo).
53. Blunderbuss, Guard's stage-coach, with spring bayonet (two).
54. Blunderbuss, Guard's stage-coach (two).
55. Swords used by Yeomen of the Guard, Irish House of Parliament, 17th century; ornamented.
(There are many others to be seen in other parts of the Hall.)
56. Blunderbuss, brass, Customs.
57. Battle-axes (three).
58. Boarding-axe.
59. Tomahawk, large.
60. Do. small.
61. French cuirass, early 19th century.
62. British armour—breastplate, black (middle of 17th century).
63. Do. —backplate do.
64. Infantry sword-bayonet, early 19th century.
65. Troopers' pistols, flint-lock, second half of 17th century.
(A number of these are to be found round the remainder of the Hall.)
66. Lances, early 19th century.
67.
68. } Muskets, flint-lock, with plug-bayonet, 1717.
69. Musket, flint-lock, with bayonet, 1727.
70. Do. do. 1731.
71. Musket, flint-lock, with mortar for throwing grenades, 1744.
72. Carbine, flint-lock, *breech-loading*, with *spear*, 1786.
73. Halberds, ancient, with spear heads
74.
75. } Carbines, flint-lock, seven-barrelled, 1786.
76. Musket, flint-lock, East India Company, 1790.
77. Carbine, flint-lock, with bayonet, heavy dragoons, 1790.
78. Rifle, flint-lock, Baker's pattern, with bayonet, 1796.

79. Rifle, flint-lock, with sword-bayonet, 1800.
80. Carbine, flint-lock, light cavalry, 1800.
81. Carbine, flint-lock, with jointed stock, light cavalry, 1800.
82. }
83. } Musketoons, ancient, first half of 17th century.
84. }
85. } Tilting Spears, similar to 14 and 15.
86. }
87. } Mortars, 5½ inch.
88. Irons in which malefactors were hung (from Fort Camden, Cork Harbour).
89. Carbine, flint-lock, rifled, 1810.
90. Carbine, flint-lock, cavalry, 1830.
91. Musket, flint-lock, altered to percussion, 1839.
92. Carbine, cavalry, percussion, Paget's, 1839.
93. Carbine, heavy cavalry, percussion, Victoria pattern, 1839.
94. Rifle, Sergeant of the Guards, 1840.
95. Rifle, Brunswick belted ball, 1841.
96. Musket, percussion, line regiments, 1842.
97. Blunderbuss, brass, Customs.
98. Wall-piece, small.
99. } Pistols, ancient flint-lock with iron stocks.
100. } Scotch. No date.
101. Helmet, ancient, graven with arms. Spanish.
(Similar to 49.)
102. }
103. } Wall-pieces ; time of George II.
104. Musket, percussion, miniature, gentleman cadet's.
105. Musket, percussion, Artillery, 1842.
106. Musket, percussion, Sappers and Miners, with bayonet, 1842.
107. Carbine, double-barrelled, Cape Corps, used by the 17th Lancers, 1847.
108. Rifle, Minie, 1851.
109. Rifle, percussion, converted from smooth bore, 1852.
110. Carbine, Lancaster, elliptical bore, 1853.
111. Rifle, Enfield, with bayonet, 1853.
112. Cuirassier's armour, 17th century.
113. Pistol, flint-lock, light cavalry, 1800.
114. Do. heavy cavalry, 1800.
115. Sword bayonets, latter end of 18th and early 19th century.
116. Rude breast-plate, trooper's, 17th century.
117. Helmet, naval, Spanish. Time of the Armada, 1588.
118. Swords, Drummers of Guards Regiments, brass-hilted, early 19th century.
119. } Mahratta Shields, with breech-loading matchlock, pistols,
120. } ancient (very curious).
121. Blunderbuss, Guards' stage-coach, with spring bayonet.
121A. Kettledrums used by the Carlow Yeomanry.
122. Pistol, flint-lock, 1702.
123. Scimitars, Light Dragoons and Artillery, 1815.
124. Swords, heavy cavalry, 1750.
125. Swords, Infantry Sergeant's, first half of 19th century.

126. Pistol, flint-lock, 1688.
127.   Do.   do.   1786.
128. Carbine, rifled, artillery, with sword bayonet, 1853.
129. Carbine, rifled, cavalry, 1856.
130. Rifle, shot, 1856, with sword bayonet.
131. Carbine, rifled, breech-loading Sharpe's, cavalry, 1857.
132. Rifle, naval, 1856, with cutlass.
133. Swords, all services, 1853.
134. Rifle, short, 1860, with sword bayonet.
135. Carbine, breech-loading, Westley Richards, 1861.
136. Rifle, Whitworth, with bayonet, 1862.
137. Rifle, muzzle-loading, converted to breech-loading on Snider principle, 1866, with bayonet.
138. Rifle, Martini-Henry, 1874.
139. Rifle, Magazine, 1890.

MODELS OF ORDNANCE ON TABLE IN NORTH EAST-CORNER

1. Light Field Piece and Carriage.
2. Heavy   do.   do.
3. Brass Garrison Gun and Carriage, 18-pounder.
4. Garrison Gun and Carriage, 24-pounder.
5.   Do.   do.   do.
6. Garrison Gun, Carriage, and Traversing Platform.
7. Howitzer and Travelling Carriage, 18-pounder.
8.   Do.   do.   do.   24-pounder.
9. Mortar and Bed, 10 inch.
10.   Do.   do.   13 inch.
11. Carronade, Platform and Slide.
12. Slide and Carriage, 18-pounder carronade.
13.   Do.   do.   24-pounder   Do.
14.   Do.   do.   32-pounder   Do.
15. Ship Carriage, sliding platform.
16.   Do.   do.   do.

ON TABLE WITH MODELS

17. One Gun, hand Grenade.
18. ⎫
19. ⎭ Two Guns, hand, fire-ball

LIST OF ARTICLES OF INTEREST PRESENTED IN RECENT YEARS TO THE ROYAL HOSPITAL, AND UNNUMBERED

Brass Guns taken by Gen. Sir Garnet Wolseley, G.C.B., etc., at the Battle of Tel-el-Keber, September 13th, 1882, presented by the Dowager Lady Wolseley.

Soudanese Jibba, taken at Omdurman, 1898, presented by Gen. the Rt. Hon. Sir N. G. Littleton, G.C.B., etc.

Gun-Carriage which bore the remains of " Her Most Excellent Majesty, Victoria, Queen of Great Britain and Ireland, Defender of the Faith, Empress of India," from Victoria Station to Paddington Station, London, on February 2nd, 1901. This gun-carriage belonged to the 109th Battery R.F.A., and has been placed for safe custody in the Royal Hospital, where it was deposited from Woolwich Arsenal in September, 1901.

" Queen Victoria " Chocolate Box, as presented by Her Majesty to the troops in South Africa, given by the Army Council, 1902.

Boer Officer's Uniform and accoutrements, presented by Field-Marshal H.R.H. the Duke of Connaught and Strathearn, K.G., etc. 1902.

Lid and Ends of a Pike Chest of great antiquity which belonged to the Order of St. John of Jerusalem, presented by Col. W. G. Collingwood, 1904.

A picture of Hannah Snell, presented by Brig. Gen. A. E. Sanbach, C.B., etc., 1911.

Print, " The Most Noble Prince, James, Duke of Ormond,'' presented by Major K. Kincaird-Smith, D.S.O., Assistant Military Secretary, Ireland, 1916.

Oil-painting of the late In-Pensioner Robert Moneypenny, VIII. Hussars, presented by the Dowager Viscountess Wolseley, April, 1919.

Arms and Armour of various periods, presented by Maj.-Gen. F. F. Ready, C.B., etc., 1920.

> 4 Rifles, 2 Suits of Armour, 2 Bandoliers, 2 Swords, 1 Revolver, 2 Helmets, 1 Brass Brow Band.

APPENDIX V

MEDALS WHICH BELONGED TO SOME FORMER INMATES, NOW EXHIBITED IN THE GREAT HALL

LIST OF MEDALS IN NO. I CASE

No.	Name.	Corps.	Description of Medals.	Clasp.
1.	Philip Aylward	18th Royal Irish	China	
2.	William Reid	Royal Artillery	Crimea	Alma, Inkerman, Sebastopol
3.	W. Wilkinson	94th Regiment	Peninsula	Toulouse, Orthes, Salamanca, Badajos, Ciudad Rodrigo, Fuentes D'Onor
4.	Henry White	1st Regiment	Burmah	Ava
5.	William Smith	52nd Regiment	Peninsula	Pyrenees Vittoria Salamanca Badajoz Ciudad Rodrigo Fuentes D'Onor Corunna

No.	Name.	Corps.	Description of Medals.	Clasps.
6.	Charles Hall	32nd Regiment	Waterloo	
7.	Michael Reilly	61st Regiment	Indian Mutiny	Delhi
8.	Daniel Cahill	56th Regiment	Crimea Turkish	Sebastopol
9.	John Glenn	18th Hussars	Peninsula Waterloo	Toulouse
10.	John Bethell	14th Regiment	Crimea Turkish	Sebastopol
11.	Frederick Kane	77th Regiment	Crimea Turkish	Alma Inkerman Sebastopol
12.	Henry Largy	47th Regiment	Burmah	Ava
13.	Patrick Burns	3rd Regiment	Crimea Turkish	Sebastopol
14.	Patrick Cavanagh	27th Regiment	South Africa, 1853	
15.	Richard Heavy	58th Regiment	Good Conduct	
16.	John Ryan	19th Regiment	N.W. Frontier	N.W. Frontier
17.	Patrick O'Connor	75th Regiment	Indian Mutiny	Lucknow Delhi
18.	Daniel Murphy	45th Regiment	South Africa	

LIST OF MEDALS IN NO. 2 CASE

No.	Name.	Corps.	Description of Medals.	Clasps.
1.	John Allan	27th Regiment	Peninsula	Pyrenees Vittoria Salamanca Badajoz
2.	John Dwyer	Royal Artillery	Indian Mutiny	Central India
3.	John Noonan	48th Regiment	Peninsula	Salamanca Badajoz Ciudad Rodrigo Albuhera
4.	John Ennis	17th Lancers	Peninsula	Badajoz Busaco Talavera Vimiera Roleia
5.	Andrew Hill	88th Regiment	Peninsula	Fuentes D'Onor
6.	Jonathan Benson	20th Light Dragoons	Peninsula	Vimiera Roleia
7.	Thomas O'Keele	31st Regiment	Crimea	Sebastopol
8.	William Neil	13th Light Infantry	Jellahabad, 42 Cabul, 42	
9.	Owen Reynolds	86th and 56th	Good Conduct	
10.	Michael Donovan	58th and 33rd	S. Africa Abyssinia	1879
11.	John O'Brien	33rd Regiment	Crimea Turkish	Alma Inkerman Sebastopol
12.	Robert Deaco.	Ambulance Corps	Crimea	Inkerman

F

No.	Name.	Corps.	Description of Medals.	Clasps.
13.	Patrick Carroll	40th Regiment	Bronze Star, Maharajpoor, 29-12-43, New Zealand	
14.	J. Maguire	Royal Artillery	Afghanistan	Ahmed Khel
15.	Daniel Maguire	46th Foot	Good Conduct	
16.	Michael Lynch	103rd Regiment	Good Conduct	
17.	Daniel Kelly	Royal Artillery	Good Conduct	
18.	Patrick Moran	13th Foot	Good Conduct	

LIST OF MEDALS IN NO. 3 CASE

No.	Name.	Corps.	Description of Medals.	Clasps.
1.	John Sullivan	Royal Artillery	Indian Mutiny Persia Good Conduct	Persia
2.	Thomas Lawton	37th Foot	Indian Mutiny	
3.	John Drohan	17th Foot	Crimea Turkish	Sebastopol
4.	Thomas Runnahan	Royal Bengal Horse Artillery	Indian Mutiny	Lucknow Relief of Lucknow Delhi
5.	Edward O'Brien	Royal Horse Artillery	Crimea Turkish Good Conduct	Sebastopol
6.	Richard Arnold	75th Foot	Indian Mutiny	Delhi
7.	Bernard Coin	8th Hussars	Crimea Indian Mutiny Turkish	Sebastopol Lucknow
8.	Joseph North	Military Police	Good Conduct	
9.	Michael Grehan	106th Foot	Persia Good Conduct	Persia
10.	John Walsh	88th Foot	Crimea	Sebastopol Inkerman Alma
11.	Edward Gorman	88th Foot	Indian Mutiny Good Conduct	Central India
12.	Patrick Kelly	87th Foot	Indian Mutiny Good Conduct	
13.	John Ryan	76th Foot	Good Conduct	
14.	James Frawley	Royal Artillery	Indian Mutiny	
15.	John Donahie	17th Foot	Crimea Turkish	Sebastopol
16.	Joseph Totten	R.C. Rifles	Fenian Raid	1866
17.	John Collopy	36th Foot	Crimea Indian Mutiny Turkish	Sebastopol

APPENDICES

No.	Name.	Corps.	Description of Medals.	Clasps.
1.	William Fox	15th Regiment	Fenian Raid	Fenian Raid
2.	John O'Brien	Royal Artillery	Turkish Crimea Good Conduct	Sebastopol
3.	Thomas Cavanagh	98th Regiment	Fenian Raid	Fenian Raid
4.	James McVey	26th Regiment	Good Conduct	
5.	Martin Slater	70th Regiment	Indian Mutiny Good Conduct New Zealand	
6.	Patrick McCann	Royal Artillery	Good Conduct	
7.	Maurice Madden	55th Regiment	Indian Mutiny Crimea Turkish Good Conduct	Sebastopol
8.	Luke Mc'Cormick	87th Regiment	Indian Mutiny	
9.	Patrick Meeney	Royal Artillery	Coronation	
10.	Joseph Mc'Neil	Leicester Regiment	Good Conduct	Sebastopol
11.	John Slevin	31st Foot	Indian Mutiny China	Taku Forts
12.	Patrick Joyce	Durham L.I.	Fenian Raid Good Conduct	Fenian Raid
13.	Thomas Lawless	Durham L.I.	New Zealand Good Conduct	
14.	Mrs. Regan	Late Head Nurse, Royal Hospital, Kilmainham	Imperial Service	
15.	James D'Arcy	86th Regiment	South Africa Cape of Good Hope Abyssinia Queen's, South Africa, King's, South Africa	1877-8-9 { Basutoland Transkei Cape Colony S.A. 1901 S.A. 1902
16	Charles Hughes	Royal Artillery	Crimea Turkish Indian Mutiny	Sebastopol

No.	Name.	Corps.	Description	Clasps.
1.	Thomas Murray	Royal Engineers	Good Conduct	
2.	John Mc'Cluskey	East Kent Regiment	Zulu Medal	

APPENDIX VI

MEDALS FOR WAR-SERVICE AND GOOD CONDUCT IN POSSESSION OF IN-PENSIONERS, NOVEMBER, 1921

						Medals.
Crimean War	..	..	..	1854-56	..	2
Turkish Medals						2
China	..	..	..	1860	..	1
Reil Rebellion	..	..	..	1865	..	2
New Zealand War		..	..	1866	..	2
Hazara	..	..	..	1868	..	3
Umbela	..	..	..		..	1
Perak	..	..	..	1875	..	1
Afghanistan	..	..	..	1879-80	..	14
Cabul-Khandhar Stars	..	..		..	..	2
Zulu War	..	..	..	1879	..	7
South Africa	..	..	..	1879	..	1
Egypt	..	..	..	1882-85	..	12
Khedive's Stars						12
Burmah	..	..	..	1887-89	..	4
Jawaki	..	..	..		..	1
Chitral	..	..	..	1895	..	1
N.W. Frontier of India	..	..	..	1897	..	4
South African War	..	..	..	1899-1902	..	
Queen's Medals						16
King's Medals						9
European War	..	..	..	1914-1918		
1914 Stars	..	..		..	..	3
General Service Medals	..	..		..	..	5
Victory Medals	..	..		..	..	5
Meritorious Medal	..	..		..	..	1
Good Conduct Medals	..	..		..	..	15
Militia Long Service Medal	..		..	..	1
Delhi Durbar Medal	..	...		..	..	1

APPENDIX VII

LIST OF MASTERS

Colonel John Jeffreys, *by Charter*	..	..	.. 1684
Colonel Daniel Venner	..	..	.. 1692
Earl of Meath	..	..	.. 1692
Sir Charles Feilding	..	..	.. 1699
Lieut.-General Palmer	..	..	.. 1714
Brigadier-General James Crofts	..	..	.. 1718
,, ,, David Crichton	..	..	.. 1719
,, ,, Robert Sterne	..	..	.. 1728
Lieut.-Colonel Philip Bragg	..	..	.. 1733
Brigadier-General Theodore Vesey	..	..	.. 1735
Colonel Wansbrough	..	..	.. 1737
,, Jasper Price	..	..	.. 1739
,, William Hall	..	..	.. 1744

Major-General Michael O'Brien Dilkes 1755
Lieut.-General John Irwin 1775
    ,,   John Burgoyne 1782
    ,,   William Augustus Pitt 1784
    ,,   George Warde 1792
    ,,   Robert Cunningham (afterwards Lord Rossmore) 1793
General the Earl of Carhampton 1796
Lieut.-General Sir Ralph Abercombie 1797
    ,,   G. Lake 1798
    ,,   the Earl of Clanricarde 1800
General Sir William Meadows 1801
Lieut.-General Hon. Henry Edward Fox 1803
General the Lord Cathcart 1803
Lieut.-General John Floyd 1806
General the Earl of Harrington 1806
General Sir John Hope 1812
General Sir George Hewitt 1813
General Sir George Beckwith 1816
General Sir David Baird 1820
General Sir Samuel Auchmutty 1822
Field-Marshal Viscount Combermere 1822
Lieut.-General Sir George Murray 1825
    ,,   Sir John Byng 1828
    ,,   Sir R. Hussey Vivian 1831
    ,,   Sir Edward Blakeney, K.B. 1835
Field-Marshal Lord Seaton, G.C.B. 1855
General Sir George Brown, G.C.B. 1860
General Lord Strathnairn, G.C.B., G.C.S.I. 1865
General Lord Sandhurst, G.C.B., G.C.S.I. 1870
General Sir John Michel, G.C.B. 1875
General Sir Thomas Steele, K.C.B. 1880
General H.S.H. Prince Edward of Saxe-Weimar, G.C.B. .. 1885
General Viscount Wolseley, K.P., G.C.B., G.C.M.G. .. 1890
Field-Marshal the Rt. Hon. the Lord Roberts, V.C., K.P.,
    G.C.B., G.C.S.I., G.C.I.E. 1895
General H.R.H. the Duke of Connaught, K.G., K.T., K.P., G.C.B.,
    G.C.S.I., G.C.M.G., G.C.I.E., G.C.V.O. 1900
General the Rt. Hon. the Lord Grenfell, G.C.B., G.C.M.G. .. 1904
General the Rt. Hon. Sir Neville Lyttleton, G.C.B., etc. .. 1908
General the Rt. Hon. Sir Arthur Paget, K.C.B., K.C.V.O. .. 1912
Major-General the Rt. Hon. L. B. Friend, C.B. 1914
Lieut.-General the Rt. Hon. Sir John Maxwell, G.C.B.,
    K.C.M.G., C.V.O., D.S.O. 1916
Lieut.-General the Rt. Hon Sir Brian Mahon, K.C.V.O.,
    C.B., D.S.O. 1916
Lieut.-General the Rt. Hon. Sir F. C. Shaw, K.C.B. .. 1918
General the Rt. Hon. Sir C. F. N. Macready, G.C.M.G.,
    K.C.B. 1920

APPENDIX VIII

" 24th June Anno 1702.

" The Annuall Charge of the Hospitall of King Charles the Second neare Dublin as the same hath been Established by the Governors thereof in respect of yᵉ Master Officers & Servants of the House & 400 Super Annuated & Disabled Souldᵣˢ now maintained in yᵉ said Hospitall and (98) allowed 18d each per Weeke in money abroad.
" Officers & Servants.   Their Offices and Services.

		Annuall Salarys		
		£	s.	d.
Sr. Charles Fielding	Master for Salary & Table ..	400	0	0
Sr. Patrick Dun	Phisition	50	0	0
John Twells Chaplaine to be Continued to him at £80 p. ann. but no succeeding Chaplaine to have more than £50 p. ann.		80	0	0
	Carried forward	£530	0	0
	Brought forward	£530	0	0
Robert Curtis	Auditor & Register	50	0	0
Ephraim Dawson	Pay Master..	50	0	0
David Ward	Ayd Major	26	0	0
Thomas Grantham	Reader	20	0	0
Wm. Partington	Chirurgeon	50	0	0
Robert Curtis, Junr.	Mate	20	0	0
Peter Goodwin	Providore	50	0	0
Tho. Baker	Apothecary	20	0	0
Andrew Goodwin	Butler	16	0	0
Tho. Hawkins	Cooke	16	0	0
Mary Hoskins	Under Cooke	8	0	0
John Hollins	Fueller & Chamber Keeper ..	16	0	0
	Carried over	£872	0	0
	Brought forward	£872	0	0
Henry Burleigh	Clerke of the Chappell ..	2	10	0
Idem	For Cleaning the Chappell ..	1	0	0
Richd. Jameson	Messenger	6	0	0
Edwd. Gent, Senr.	Sculleryman	12	0	0
Edwd. Gent, Junr.	His Assistant	8	0	0
James Davis } Jone Ellis }	Helpers in yᵉ Kitchen ..	5	0	0
Daniel Walsh	Waterman without Dyet ..	16	18	0
Christ. Livelock	Hall Keeper	6	0	0
David Boyde }	.. .. ..	16	18	0
John Rice }	Porters without Dyet ..	16	18	0
Edwd. Branthwaite }	.. ..	16	18	0
	Carried forward	£980	2	0

		Annuall Salarys		
		£	s.	d.
	Brought forward	980	2	0
Gilbert Mines	Porter without Dyet ..	16	18	0
Abigall Bridges	.. ..	6	10	0
Elinor Delapp	.. ..	6	10	0
Eliz. Laurence	.. ..	6	10	0
Jennet Tremble	.. ..	6	10	0
Mary Graham	Nurses	6	10	0
Eliz. McCullogh	.. .. ..	6	10	0
Jennet Brown	.. ..	6	10	0
Elz. Ward	.. ..	6	10	0
Mary Hayes	.. ..	6	10	0
Mary Hughes	.. ..	6	10	0
	Carried over	£1062	0	0
	Brought forward	£1062	0	0
Elinor Hinard	.. .. ..	6	10	0
Susanna Williams	Nurses	6	10	0
Rose Rayner	.. ..	2	0	0
Lt. Walter Jones	.. .. ..	10	0	0
Qr. Mr. Hen. Fletcher	.. .. ..	10	0	0
Lt. Henry Higdon	Decayed Officers	10	0	0
Qr. Mr. Ja. Galbraith	..	10	0	0
Lt. John Daniel	.. .. ..	10	0	0
Qr. Mr. Lewis Jones	.. .. ..	10	0	0
Thomas Elliot	Clock Keeper	10	0	0
	Carried forward	£1139	10	0

	£	s.	d.
Brought forward	£1139	10	0
Undertaker of the Slateing Worke of the Hospitall	18	0	0
Andrew Rock Undertaker of ye Glasing Worke	24	0	0
Mrs. Frances Goodwin Undertaker of ye Washing of the Soulders' Linnen, Sheets, Table Linnen, &c., for 400 men at 15s. each	300	0	0
Incident Charges to be accompted for by Mr. Peter Goodwin	70	0	0
Mr. Francis Baker Apothecary for Medicaments for 400 Men at 2s. 6d. each p. ann.	50	0	0
Carried forward	£1601	10	0
Brought forward	£1601	10	0
Three Barbers for Shaveing the Souldiers once a weeke at £3 each p. ann.	9	0	0
To a Labourer for Workeing in the Garden ..	7	0	0
To Mr. Peter Goodwin (by Contract) for ye Dyet of 400 Souldiers at 3d. ¼ p. diem for each man ..	1977	1	8
To him more for the Dyet of 24 Inferior Officers & Servants of ye Hospitall at 4d. p. diem each ..	146	0	0
To him more for the Dyet of six Decayed Officers at £12 p. ann. each	72	0	0
Carried forward	£3812	11	8

				Annuall Salarys		
				£	s.	d.
Brought forward	..	..		38 12	11	8
Tobacco Money for 400 Souldiers at two pence p.						
Weeke each			..	173	6	8
Addiconall Tobacco Money of two pence p. Weeke						
each to 8 Serg^{ts} doeing duty at ye Hospitall			..	3	9	4
Cloathing for 400 Sould^{rs}. (viz.)						
Coate and Wastcoate for each man once in						
two Yeares at £1 9s. 9d. of which one						
halfe to be Charged as ye yearly						
Expence		..	0 14 10½			
1 payre of Breeches		..	0 5 0			

			0 19 10½			
Carried over ..		..		3989	7	8

Brought over ..		..		3989	7	8
1 Hatt ..	..	..	0 3 9			
1 payre of Stockens	..	..	0 1 4			
2 Shirts ..	..	..	0 7 0			
1 Cravatt ..	..	..	0 1 8			
1 payre of Shooes	..	..	0 4 0			
2 Linnen Capps	..	..	0 1 6			

			1 19 1½			
Which for 400 Men makes yearly..		..		782	10	0
For 260 Tuns of Sea-Coales at 15s. 6d. per tun &						
2s. 6d. p. tun for Carriage thereof to the Hospitall				234	0	0
For 716 Barrells of Char: Coale at 2s. p. Barrell		..		71	12	0
Carried forward ..		..		5077	9	8

Brought forward	..	..		5077	9	8
For 260 Doz. and 6 1½ of Candles at 3s. 10d. per. doz				49	18	9
For Oyle for 4 Lamps or Convex lights at ye Hospitall						
and Cotton		..		4	15	0
To 98 Old and Disabled Souldiers who quitted y^e						
Hospitall for an allow^{ce.} of 18d. p. Weeke each						
in money without Cloathes ..		..		382	4	0
				5514	7	5

Added Since.

To Ensn. Julius Caesar Admitted as a Decay'd						
Office^r from ye 3^d Augt 1702 by Order dated						
ye 10th Septemb^r foll. (viz.)		..	..			
For Cloathes	..	..	..			
For Dyet ..	..	..	..			
				22	0	0
				£5536	7	5

APPENDIX IX

DISPOSAL OF LAND

	A.	R.	P
Under Main Building and grounds	5	1	37
Under Infirmary and Grounds, Gardens and Laundry	3	1	12
Military Road Field	6	1	3
Western Avenue	1	3	31
Burial ground	0	1	3
" Bully's Acre "	2	0	33
Master's Fields	11	1	28
Deputy Master's Fields	2	0	9
Master's Garden	3	0	29
Deputy Master's Garden	0	1	24
New Stables	0	1	22½
Island Bridge Barracks	2	2	0
Conveyed to Great Southern and Western Railway	21	2	5½
	60	3	37

The Military road, St. John's road, a piece of ground which adjoined " Bully's Acre," and a piece of ground cut off in making the South Circular Road, make up the sixty-four acres granted by the Charter.

Commanders of the Forces in Ireland with the Principal

Year.	Commander of the Forces	Military Secretary	Adjutant General
1801, 10 June	Gen. Sir Wm. Meadows, K.B.	—	Col. Hon. Alex. Hope Brig.-Gen. Robert Anstruther
1803, 1 June	Lt.-Gen. Henry Ed. Fox	Colonel Beckwith	do.
1803, 16 Oct.	Lt.-Gen. Lord Cathcart	do. Lt.-Col. Jas. Kirkman	do.
1805, 31 Oct.	Gen. the Earl of Harrington	Col. H. M. Gordon	do. Brig.-Gen. Henry Clinton
1812, 25 Jan.	Lt.-Gen. Sir John Hope	Lt.-Col. John Macdonald	Maj.-Gen. Jas. Hay
1813, 25 Sept.	Gen. Sir Geo. Hewett, Bart.	Col. Peter Carey	do. Maj.-Gen. Sir Geo. Murray Maj.-Gen. Lord Aylmer, K.C.B.
1816, 10 Oct.	Gen. Sir Geo. Beckwith, G.C.B.	do.	do.
1820, 25 Mar.	Gen. Sir David Baird, G.C.B.	Lt.-Col. T. S. Sorell	do.
1822, 25 June	Lieut.-Gen. Sir Samuel Auchmuty, G.C.B. (Died on 11 Aug., 1822)	do.	**Assistant Military Secretary.**
1822, 25 Oct.	Lt.-Gen. Lord Combermere, G.C.B.	Maj. Hon. John Finch	Lt. Henry M'Manus, from 1801 to 1825
1825, 25 Mar.	Lieut.-Gen. Sir George Murray, G.C.B.	Lt.-Col. Wedderburn	do.
1828, 9 June	Lt.-Gen. Sir John Byng, K.C.B	Lt.-Col. the Earl of Wiltshire Lt.-Col. Sir Fred. Stovin, K.C.B.	Lieut. Wm. Siborn do.
1831, 1 July	Lt.-Gen. Sir R. Hussey, Bart, K.C.B.	Lieut.-Col. Lord Templemore Capt. Vivian, 7 Huss. Lt.-Col. A. Cuyler	do.
1836, 26 Aug.	Lieut.-Gen. Sir Edward Blakeney, K.C.B.	Maj. Greaves, 34th Regt.	do. Capt. F. Murray, 60th Rifles Capt. Hon. C. Forester, 12th Lancers Maj. Hon. St. G. Foley Capt. Hillier, 53rd Regt. Capt. Blakeney, 48th Foot
1855, 12 Mar.	General Lord Seaton, G.C.B.	Maj. Hon. J. Colborne	—
1860, 1 April	Gen. Sir Geo. Brown, G.C.B.	Lt.-Col. E. A. Whitmore	—
1865, 1 July	Gen. Sir Hugh Rose, G.C.B., G.C.S.I. (afterwards Lord Strathnairn)	Lt.-Col. Hon. Leicester (Curzon) Smyth, C.B.	—
1870, 1 Aug.	Lieut.-Gen. Sir W. R. Mansfield, G.C.B. (afterwards Lord Sandhurst)	—	Col. E. Fellowes, Lt.-Col. G. N. Fendall, 53rd Foot

Officers of their Staff in succession from the year 1801.

Deputy Adjutant General	Quarter-Master General	Deputy Qr.-Master General	Commanding Royal Artillery.
Col. W. Raymond	Maj.-Gen. Cradock	Col. T. Brownrigg	—
do.	do.	do.	—
do.	do.	do.	—
do.	Maj.-Gen. Clinton	Col. Geo. Murray	—
	do.	do.	—
Lieut.-Col. Nicols	Maj.-Gen. George Murray	Lt.-Col. Samuel Brown	—
Lt.-Col. Peter Carey			
Col. R. A. Dalzell	Maj. Gen. Airy	do.	—
Col. John Ross			
do.	do.	—	Col. Sir Haylett Framingham (for a short time)
Col. Wm. Thornton, C.B.			
do.	do.	do.	—
do.	Commanding Royal Engineer.	do.	—
do.	—	do.	—
Col. Gardiner, C.B.			
do.	—	Col. Sir James Douglas, K.C.B.	—
do.	—	do.	—
Col. D'Aguilar		Col. Sir Guy Campbell, Bart.	
do.	—	do.	Col. Sir Ths. Downman, K.C.B.
do.	Col. Arnold	do.	Col. Webber Smith, C.B.
Col. P. F. Wade, C.B.	Lt.-Col. W. C. E. Holloway	Col. P. Bainbrigge, C.B.	Col. Munro, K.H.
Col. T. E. Napier	Col. G. G. Lewis	Col. Mansell, K.H.	Col. G. Turner, C.B.
Col. Cochrane	Col. W. H. Vavasour	Col. J. L. Pennefather, C.B.	Col. Thos. Dyneley
Col. John Eden, C.B.	Col. J. Oldfield, K.H.	Col. J. B. Gough	Col. W. B. Dundas, C.B.
Col. W. F. Forster, K.H.	Col. A. Emmett		Col. T G. Higgins
Col. R. B. Woods, C.B.	Col. A. Emmett	Col. R. Greaves	Col. T. G. Higgins
Col. J. S. Brownrigg, C.B.	Col. C. Rose	Col. E. R. Weatherall	
	Col. Ed. Froine	Col. J. S. Brownrigg, C.B.	
	—	Col. E. R. Weatherall, C.B.	
do.	—	do.	Col. J. W. Ormsby
Col. F. P. Haines		Col. E. A. Somerset, B.C.	Col. J. W. Fitzmayer
Col. K. D. Mackenzie, C.B.			Col. G. J. L. Buchanan
do.	—	do.	do.
Col. F. W. Armstrong, C.B.		Col. G. W. Mayow, C.B.	Col. T. B. F. Marriott
			Col. R. P. Radcliffe
Col. J. M. Primrose, C.S.I.	Col. J. S. Hawkins	do.	do.
Col. Sir Arch. Alison, Bart, K.C.B.	Col. T. A. L. Murray	Col. Hon. Leicester Smyth, C.B.	Col. C. B. Fuller
		Col. H. H. Crealock, C.B.	

Commanders of the Forces in Ireland, with the Principal

Year	Commander of the Forces	Military Secretary	Assistant Military Secretary
1875, 2 Aug.	Gen. Sir John Michel, G.C.B.	—	Lieut.-Col. C. A. Wynne-Finch, Scots Fus. Gds. Lt.-Col. Hon. Paul Methuen, Scots Fus. Guards Lt.-Col. Hon. E. Boscawen, Coldstream Guards
1880, 1 Oct.	Gen. Sir Thomas M. Steele, K.C.B.	—	Col. P. D. Boyle, Grenr. Guards
1885, 1 Oct.	Gen. H.S.H. Prince Ed. of Saxe-Weimar, G.C.B.	—	Lt.-Col. A. E. Turner, R.A. Maj. C. E. Beckett, 3rd Huss. Capt. W. H. Darby, R.A.
1890, 1 Oct.	Gen. Viscount Wolseley, K.P., G.C.B., G.C.M.G.	—	Major E. S. E. Childers, R.E.
		Assist. Military Secretary.	**Deputy Adjutant General.**
1895, 1 Oct.	Field-Marshal Lord Roberts	Maj. H. Streatfield, Grenr. Guards Maj. H. V. Cowan, R.A.	Col. W. F. Kelly Col. R. L. H. Curteis
1900, 9 Jan.	Gen. H.R.H. Duke of Connaught and Strathearn (Commanding IIIrd Army Corps)	Maj. M. McNeill, R. of O. Bt. Lt.-Col. W. N. Congreve, R.B.	Col. A. G. Wavell **Chief Staff Officer** Brig.-Gen. Sir J. G. Maxwell (Nov. '02)
1904, 10 May	Field-Marshal Lord Grenfell	Maj. G. S. St. Aubyn, K.R.R.C. Maj. L. F. Philips, K.R.R.C.	Brig.-Gen. Hon. A. H· Henniker, Major **Brig.-Gen. Gen. Staff** Brig.-Gen. F. Hanmersley Brig.-Gen. Sir C. Fergusson, Bart.
1908, 10 May	Gen. Sir N. G. Lyttelton	Bt.-Col. G. H. Thesiger, R.B. Lt.-Col. Hon. H. Yarde-Buller, R.B.	Brig.-Gen. E. S. May Brig.-Gen. K. F. N. McCracken
1912, 10 May	Lt.-Gen. Sir A. Paget	Maj. K. S. Kincaid-Smith, R.A.	Brig.-Gen. G. T. Forestier-Walker

Officers of their Staff in succession from the year 1801.

Deputy Adjutant General	Quarter-Master General	Deputy Qr.-Master General	Commanding Royal Artillery
Col. Sir Arch. Alison, Bart., K.C.B.	Col. T. A. L. Murray	Col. H. H. Crealock, C.B.	Col. C. B. Fuller
Col. G. B. Harman	Col. H. Wray, C.M.G.	Col. T. C. Lyons, C.B.	—
		Col. Sir T. D. Baker, K.C.B.	
do.	do.	do.	
Col. Sir T. D. Baker, K.C.B.	Col. W. H. Noble	Col. H. D. Maclean	—
Col. N. Stevenson		Col. H. J. Buchanan, C.B.	
do.	do.	do.	—
Col. C. M. Clarke, C.B.	Col. W. D. Marsh	Col. B. L. Foster	Maj.-Gen. Johnson, C.B.
Col. W. L. Dalrymple	Col. F. A. Le Mesurier	Col. J. Duncan	Maj.-Gen. LeCocq
do.	do.	**Assistant Adjutant General.**	do.
Col. J. Duncan		Col. J. Talbot Coke	do.
Col. W. R. Lascelles			
Assistant Adjutant General.	**Assist. Quarter-Master General.**	**Commanding Royal Engineer.**	
Col. J. Talbot Coke		Col. F. A. Le Mesurier	do.
		Chief Engineer.	
		Col. R. Vetch	
Col. E. S. Courtenay		do.	
Col. J. Davidson			
Col. A. E. Codrington	Col. J. Davidson	Col. C. F. C. Beresford	Maj.-Gen. Sir W. G. Knox
Col. F. Hammersley		Col. E. Dickenson	
do.			
Brig.-Gen. i/c Administration.	Col. F. Waldron		do.
Brig.-Gen. Hon. A. H. Henniker, Major (1905)			
Maj.-Gen. i/c Administration.		Col. F. Rainsford-Hannay	(Appt. abolished)
Maj.-Gen. H. N. Bunbury (1907)			
Maj.-Gen. C. A. Hadfield	Col. W. B. Hickie	Col. C. V. Wingfield-Strafford	**S.O.Horse & Field Artillery**
Col. S. Bogle Smith (A.A.G.)			Col. J. W. Hawkins
Maj.-Gen. L. B. Friend (1913)		Brig.-Gen. A. E. Sandbach	(Appt. abolished)
Lt.-Col. F. J. de Gex (A.A.G.)	Lt.-Col. R. H. Carr Ellison		

Commanders of the Forces in Ireland, with the Principal

Year	Commander of the Forces	Assist. Military Secretary	Brig.-Gen. General Staff.
1914, 3 Sept.	Maj.-Gen. L. B. Friend (temp.) G.O.C. Troops in Ireland	Lt.-Col. R. H. F. W. Wilson, R. of O.	Brig.-Gen. R. M. Grenfield
1916, 28 April.	Lt.-Gen. Sir John G. Maxwell	do.	do.
			Brig.-Gen. R. Hutchison
		Capt. Marquess of Anglesey, R.H.G.	
1916, 15 Nov.	Lt.-Gen. Sir Brian T. Mahon	do.	do.
			Brig.-Gen. L. S. Perceval Brig.-Gen. F. H. G. Stainton
1918, 13 May	Lt.-Gen. Sir F. C. Shaw	Maj. K. S. Robertson, R. Scots	Brig.-Gen. Lord Lock
			Brig.-Gen. J. E. S. Brind
1920, 14 April.	Gen. Sir C. F. N. Macready.	do.	Col. on Staff, Gen. Staff Col. J. E. S. Brind
		Capt. R. F. Nation, Roy. Fus.	

Officers of their Staff in succession from the year 1801.

Adjutant General's Staff	Assist. Quarter-Master General.	Commanding Royal Engineer.	
Lt.-Col. F . J. de Gex (A.A.G.) Col. H. V. Cowan (A.A.G.)	Lt.-Col. R. H. Carr Ellison	Col. H. V. Kent Brig.-Gen. J. R. Young	
do.	do.	do.	
Brig.-Gen. J. A. Byrne (Dept. A.G.) Col. H. V. Cowan (A.A.G.)	do.	do.	
do. **Maj.-Gen. i/c Administration.** Maj.-Gen. W. Fry		Brig.-Gen. A. Grant	
Lt.-Col. C. H. Haig (A.A.G.)	do.	do.	
do. **Maj.-Gen. i/c Administration.** Maj.-Gen. F. F. Ready	do. Bt. Lt.-Col. H. Findlay	Brig.-Gen. W. B. Brown	**Brig.-Gen. R.A.** Brig.-Gen. C. Prescott-Decie
do. Maj.-Gen. Sir W. H. Rycroft	do.	do.	(Appt. abolished)
Appointment Maj.-Gen. i/c Administration temporarily vacant, duties vested in :—			
Depty. Adjt. Gen. Col. J. B. Wroughton	**Depty. Qr.-Mr. Gen.** Col. E. Evans	Col. G. Walker(1921)	

Lightning Source UK Ltd.
Milton Keynes UK
UKOW052250261011

181012UK00001B/12/A